FOOTBALL

TO HELP MAINTAIN the name of the Warren Symcox Childhood Development Centre part of the proceeds of sales of this book will be donated to the Sinothando Home, Galeshewe, Kimberley, to assist the children suffering from HIV and Aids.

Photographs provided by courtesy of De Beers Mines Ltd and the Kimberley Africana Library

By the Same Author

Life Down t'Lane
Memories of Tapton House School
A History of Tapton House

Email: len@sportsdraw.co.uk

ISBN 978-0-9525678-3-7
Published 2008 by
Bannister Publications
118 Saltergate, Chesterfield, Derbyshire S40 1NG
Printed and bound in Great Britain
by MPG Biddles Ltd, King's Lynn, Norfolk

Foreword

I HAVE NO DOUBT that the many emigrants to South Africa or those associated with mining will enjoy reading this book, which will bring back many memories, as well as part of the history, of Anglo American Corporation and De Beers. Those fortunate enough to have been in the De Beers Kimberley precinct were forever touched, shaped and scarred in some way. Somehow, it all seemed so right. The world beyond was a different place.

It says much for those such as Cecil Rhodes and the Oppenheimers who established and made De Beers what it is today that the precepts of the original charter permeate the company. The global giant that was born out of the dry dust of the Northern Cape, and whose Head Office still stands proudly in a quaint back street just a stone's throw away from the biggest man-made hole on planet earth, was surely responsible for shaping the lives of millions.

The Kimberley mines no longer operate under the De Beers banner and others have been closed for some years. Therefore, it is perhaps timely to gather together the many thoughts and reminiscences of some of the characters who worked and played there in an era when the diamond meant so much to so many and loyalty to the De Beers brand was life itself.

The De Beers Country Club, as one would expect, served as a "second home" to the men of the mining brotherhood. Moreover, it afforded the characters of Kimberley the opportunity to express themselves in the "Pick 'n Shovel Bar" or at any of the many grand sporting facilities provided.

Perhaps the first link between Len and me was made in 1968 when Len met my uncle, Weston, who worked in the drawing office at De Beers Head Office; this led, inevitably, to an introduction to my dad, Rodger.

My own memories are of his sons Leon, a similar age to me, and Andrew, who we always enjoyed playing with at the De Beers Country Club and our respective homes. Even though many years have passed since the time when De Beers seemed to be Kimberley itself, I still have, in my mind's eye, the boyish-looking Len Thompson, playing bowls with my father, uncles and, even, me.

To Len, his wife Iris and his family, I hope the sparkle of Kimberley and De Beers remains as bright as that diamond found by a young lad on the De Beers' farm all those years ago, and that your journey through this book is enjoyed as much by all those who choose to read it.

Patrick Leonard Symcox

Introduction

A LIFE-THREATENING ACCIDENT in 1964 saw me move lock, stock and barrel with my wife and family thousands of miles to a country we knew little about and to a lifestyle we could only have dreamed of.

This book records my recollection of our family life, places, holidays and events - both memorable and mundane. I worked at a gold mine and several diamond mines in South Africa and my aim has been to paint a picture of industrial and social life in that great country

The book is, first of all, dedicated to my children who will be able to reflect on the marvellous experiences they had in South Africa. Secondly, it is dedicated to four of our dear friends in South Africa who are no longer with us but their spirits will still be there.

Introductory Note

On February 14, 1961 the rand replaced the South African pound as the South African monetary unit, where 2 rand = 1 South African pound. The latest rate is approximately 14 rand to £1.

Conversions of most weights and measures are provided but for any that I have missed please refer to *http://www.convert-me.com/en/*

Len Thompson October 2008.

Contents

Chapter One

Personal Background: 1964-1966

OUR LIVES HOLD MANY SURPRISES and mine has been no exception. A near-death experience in February 1964 was the catalyst that helped to inspire me into making a decision to look for new opportunities overseas for myself, my wife Iris, and our two young sons Leon and Andrew.

In that month I was aged 25 and engaged on a project in Chelford, Cheshire, close by the Jodrell Bank Radio Telescope station operated by Manchester University. I didn't own a car then and had to get a lift from a colleague from the Sheepbridge Engineering Contracts department, where I worked as a contracts engineer. He delivered me to the client's offices, to supervise the installation of bunker equipment for their sand quarry.

After being dropped off I was left to use my own initiative. One of the first priorities was to organise transport to and from the quarry for myself, and three construction workers, including Bill Cooper, the chief erector. We had hired a mobile crane to be on site to offload the equipment for the project and I was told by the driver he had already booked himself in at decent digs at a pub in a village close to the site. He was kind enough to offer us all a lift to the pub after work and we set off on a route that would take us past the radio telescopes of Jodrell Bank. After about half a mile the driver had to negotiate a 90 degree bend in the road immediately in front of the telescopes. He misjudged the corner, possibly looking at the enormous mechanical structures, and hit a grassy verge next to the road. He lost control of the mobile crane, which then travelled down

1

a steepish bank, through a hawthorn hedge into a ploughed field and overturned, the vehicle hitting the earth with crushing force.

Bill and I, who were travelling on the crane, underneath the horizontal jib, were thrown and were trapped in the soft earth as the vehicle turned over, the body and the crane jib hurtling towards us. It all happened so fast: I could hear the crunch, looked up and there's this jib flying towards me. It missed my head by a matter of inches but so close that the startling image stayed with me for years. I was extremely fortunate to be unscathed. If I had jumped too far I would have been hit by the jib as it came down and bounced as it hammered into the soft ground and if I had not been thrown far enough I would have shared a similar fate as poor Bill, whose ankle was caught by the body of the crane and crushed into the soft soil. He was lucky it was furrowed soil and not hard earth or concrete, otherwise he would have lost the lower part of his leg.

Hours later, the shock of the episode started to show and I began to shake. I told myself it could have been far worse but it was the short-term memory that frightened me; the reminder of just how close to the edge we are in life, always, at every second. However, there is a saying that 'fate dictates everything'. But fate is not an exact science. It is having faith in destiny which can be a tapestry of happenings. Fate dictated that I should be brought up in a two-up two-down house in a working-class area with lots of community spirit. Somehow I managed to pass my 11 plus examination and was fortunate enough to go to a grammar school. This was partly responsible for my later successes and set me up for the life I have led ever since. My wife Iris and I are now proud parents of three children and seven grandchildren and thank God for the fate that has been bestowed upon us.

Back to the accident and its aftermath. I had to walk back to the quarry to phone for an ambulance for Bill, and a taxi to take us to the lodgings. Bill was taken by ambulance to a nearby hospital and later, when I went to visit him there, we got talking about other events in his life. This included time spent in Tanganyika, now Tanzania, when he worked for Williamsons Diamond Mines (part of the De Beers group, which I was to join later). He told me lots of stories about Africa, which whet my appetite for adventure and made me start thinking about doing something along similar lines. This talk with Bill convinced me I had to see the world, or as much as I could, before fate decided otherwise. At the end of that fateful week I was called back home because Iris had just had a miscarriage - the worst week of my life.

More than a year later, in the winter of 1965, I remembered those tales related by Bill when I was ill in bed recovering from bronchitis. I was reading an engineering magazine when I saw an advert from Anglo American Corporation (AAC) wanting experienced engineers for its gold mines in South Africa. It described a land bordered by 2,500 miles (4023 kms) of beautiful coastline and sandy beaches, where the sun shone for 90% of the time and where the cost of living was far cheaper than in the UK. It also highlighted the wildlife in the National Parks and the future prosperity through gold and diamond mining, a challenge which I relished. A series of irresistible temptations.

My instant reaction was to contact AAC and I soon had my CV prepared, based primarily on my experience working with Sheepbridge Engineering on various mines in the UK and my excellent results gained in June 1962 after a four-year Higher National Diploma course in Mechanical Engineering. The diploma had been awarded by the Institute of Mechanical Engineers in conjunction with the Ministry of Education after an approved full-time course at Chesterfield College of Technology. Not bad for a lad from Down t'Lane. At this point I think I should explain this statement.

I was brought up in a small community in Henry Street (Pot Lane) in Chesterfield, Derbyshire, during and after the Second World War. It was a struggle that took place in the days of rationing and relative poverty. I was a descendent of large families; my mam was one of 23 and my dad one of eight children. I remember events that happened inside our close-knit community, in Pot Lane, the colourful characters within it, and some of the different activities that appear to have been forgotten in today's environment. Mining was the main industry in the area and gambling was very much a way of life. The fact that I was in a position to emigrate to South Africa to a post with one of the leading mining houses in the world was a tribute to the people who helped me to get where I was in 1966.

My childhood and that of the rest of our family was scarred by poverty, which we were able to convert into a strength. It was mostly due to my mam, who had brought us up to be honest and respectable citizens. I had learnt over the years, (after a few misdemeanours), to be hard-working and thrifty. We were advised to 'look after the pennies and the pounds will look after themselves'. We weren't a particularly religious family, but were expected to do the right thing.

Mam never had much money left over to clothe us. Now and again she would join a neighbour's clothing club, paying back over many weeks, but this wasn't often, since she always preferred to pay cash. Mostly we relied on jumble sales and sometimes someone would give her a few outgrown odds and ends. This changed to a certain extent when I passed my 11-plus to go to Tapton House Grammar School. Everyone had to have a school uniform, even down to the correct colour and quality shoes and socks. Since we could not afford to pay for new clothes it meant going to the council for a grant.

I can only remember one other person at school who had to rely on grants for clothing and it certainly had a psychological effect on me. But, I will always be grateful to my mam for the way she supported me through my education, at all levels. As far as I can remember, I used to have a clothing grant every two years and I certainly needed it, when you consider having to have at least one blazer, shirts, trousers, socks, shoes and even a raincoat and satchel.

Apart from that particular occasion, in order to supplement the money coming in, to ensure we were clothed and fed, mam needed to scrimp and save every penny and used to peg rugs for other people, among other things. This entailed opening up hessian sacks that originated from a rag and bone yard and joining the sacking material into a square or rectangle, to the size of the rug required. This was then sewn all the way around the perimeter of the material to add strength at the edges. Mam would then stretch this out on the floor and strike quite intricate geometrical patterns using a blue dye and items such as plates for the circles, lengths of string to strike arcs and all sorts of implements to finalise the design which was eventually produced on the hessian.

The next step was to cut up strips of cloth of three inch by one inch material made from old clothes normally from the rag and bone shop, which were then folded and forced through the sacking, using a steel, wooden clothes or aluminium peg. The peg was probably an inch in diameter and approximately six inches long which was turned to a point to enable mam to thread the rag through the sacking and produce her work of art. Making full use of a variety of cloth, she would produce what was to me an excellent work of art, with various coloured flowers on a black or blue background. She used to make these rugs for money, or to barter with next door neighbours for items to eat or to wear or the butcher for meat. Apart from rugs for the hearth, she did rugs for the butcher's car for him to put his feet on instead of the normal rubber or plastic sheet. As my daughter Julia reminds me, the rug being pegged would go over your knees to keep you warm on a cold winter's evening!

With dad being on the dole (out of work) we did not have to pay for our school meals, but we also had to suffer the indignity of attending the school during holidays along with other 'poor boys' to obtain our free dinners. Claiming free dinners was unnecessarily cruel. It was humiliating. Somehow it appeared to be a great sin to be poor. The main beneficiary of this arrangement was mam, who at least didn't have to worry about where the money was coming from for one meal a day.

Dad was a good-looking chap and had been married before; although I honestly cannot remember it ever having been mentioned at home because of the moral code attached to failed marriages then. I have only learnt about it from other people in later years, including my half-sister Mary from his first marriage. I can't remember my dad talking about his own childhood either: it was never mentioned and remained a bit of a mystery which has been pieced together from what other people have told me. Being a serious athlete in his early years, he used to be quite slim, but, as the years progressed and my mam's cooking took its toll plus the lack of exercise, he weighed about 16 stone (101kg) and had a 17.5 inch (44 cm) shirt collar during the period in question. He was very strict at home and knew how to dish out punishment when required. His main problem was trying to control his temper, which frequently flared up for no apparent reason. The only person able to control him was mam, who would always stand up to him on our behalf, if required. Outside the home he was a different person. Apart from my mam, I have never found anyone who would say a bad word about him. He was always jovial, acknowledged the ladies in a formal but friendly manner and was never stuck for a joke or few kind words for the recipient. His nickname was Cocky Thompson and I was young Cocky.

He used to have a good voice and when he was in the mood used to serenade mam, normally when he was shaving before going out to the pub, with such songs as 'A Paper Doll' or 'The Ring My Mother Wore'. In the right mood, dad whistled like a bird, little trills up and down breaking into his songs, probably imitating the caged birds he kept, linnets, goldfinch and even a bullfinch. It was a joy to listen to. You hardly ever hear anyone whistling now, unless at a football match; is it a forgotten art? It was probably listening to my dad that drove me to learn how to whistle. After months of practice I learnt how to make a shrill noise, without fingers, and by curling my tongue into a curved shape could generate a very loud whistle; very good for attracting the girls as a wolf-whistle in the old days.

My parents had met in Chesterfield and lived together for some years before marrying in 1946 without much fanfare owing to the post-war scene of food and clothes rationing.

So that was part of my background and gives you an idea of where I was coming from when I had to make my decision regarding emigration. I was probably one of the few to break the mould by emigrating to South Africa in my late twenties, but I am sure that my background of Pot Lane and its ups and downs had a big effect on my level-headedness throughout my career and lifetime.

The bumps of childhood also taught me that the best way to survive was through optimism and cheerfulness. I learned the positive strengths of self-discipline and humour, the ability to laugh at life, which was absolutely essential in the raw framework of growing up.

In summer, as children, our great journey and climax of the year would be when mam and dad took us to Cleethorpes, Skegness, Manchester Belle Vue or, later on, Blackpool. This would only be for a day's outing, normally organised by one of the local pubs or clubs. The majority of people in the street went with us on the bus. We could now look forward, especially our children, to holidays in exotic places like Cape Town, Durban, Port Elizabeth, East London and the game parks such as the Kruger National.

When we had been to the zoo and circuses in the UK during our early years, I was never impressed by the condition of the animals. Everyone tried to be there at feeding time and it was a bit of a squash, but most animals were a big disappointment. I had been expecting lions, tigers and elephants comparable with those seen on the films in our local cinema. The ones we saw at the zoo were completely different, looking very sleepy and listless and obviously missing their normal habitat. The monkeys were constantly scratching and spent most of the time picking fleas off each other, instead of swinging from branch to branch as seen in the Tarzan films. Familiar with small creatures like newts, sticklebacks, tadpoles and frogs which we all enjoyed and gave us tremendous sport, we were looking forward to seeing many more varied animals from elephant and lions down to snakes and scorpions; especially Leon and Andrew.

Anglo American were impressed enough by my curriculum vitae to offer me an interview in London. So, in February 1966 I travelled to London by train, with copies of my CV and diploma, for the meeting at the AAC head office. Whilst on the train, I prepared my list of motivation and reasons for doing the job, as well as explaining why our family was looking forward to working and living in that country.

During the interview I asked about the salary; what other documents the family needed besides our passports and when a decision might be made about employing me. I also requested more details about the job offer, which was ambiguous to say the least. Afterwards I realised the reasons for the ambiguity. The position of engineering assistant was mainly a holding role until I had passed the Engineer's Ticket which, based on my HND results would be fairly straightforward. Once I had the certificate, my salary would increase dramatically and my job description detailed in accordance with South African law for mines and works.

I also told the interviewers I intended to read as much as possible about the country before leaving for South Africa. As promised, I worked on the idea of emigrating to South Africa and began to read everything I could find on the country. By the time we arrived there I knew far more than most people visiting somewhere for the first time. I think this was how I initially fell in love with South Africa - through all those books, even before we had set foot on African soil.

Anglo's doctors examined me and I presumably passed with flying colours as I was offered a job at Welkom Gold Mine in the

Orange Free State Province, South Africa as an engineering assistant. To be honest I never wanted to work in mining, but somehow the fates conspired that I follow in the footsteps of my Grandad Smith and many of my uncles. After all that was what men did in mining areas for generation after generation, from the birth of the industrial revolution.

I accepted their offer and this set the wheels in motion for planning our trip to South Africa. The health care on offer as part of the package was of particular importance because after the company medical I suffered severe back problems. Several X-rays at Chesterfield Royal hospital did not uncover any major problem and the trouble was diagnosed as fibrositis. When I told the doctor I was emigrating to South Africa he said that was the best thing I could do, to lie in the hot sun and let that provide the care and possible cure. Another plus point from the health point of view was my asthma/bronchitis problem. One of the books I had read referred to an Englishman who had suffered badly from severe chest problems with the damp weather in the UK. He also had a recommendation from his doctor to go to live in the dry atmosphere prevalent in Bloemfontein in the Orange Free State. He followed his doctor's suggestion and moved to Bloemfontein, approximately 86 miles (138 kms) from Welkom. Within 12 months he was able to walk up the hilly parts of the city without any wheezing at all. He was cured of his chest complaints.

Chapter Two

Emigration to South Africa and journey: September 1966

AND SO; THE DIE WAS CAST. We had become irrevocably committed to the South African adventure which follows.

Since we wanted as many of our household possessions as we could take to South Africa, for costs and familiarity reasons, preparation for packing our home into ten wooden cases got underway. I had a good friend in the carpenters' shop at Sheepbridge who provided me with all the timber required for housing the items from old stock and off-cuts, which saved me and AAC quite a lot of money in removal costs. There were also vaccinations for yellow fever and smallpox to organise, as well as finding out more about emigration and the conditions in South Africa.

There were a lot of people who I had to say cheerio to. Many of the friends I worked with expressed concern when I told them I was emigrating to South Africa. They asked why I wanted to leave the excellent job I had at Sheepbridge to go to a country where there was so much trouble. One colleague, Fred West, had left the firm to emigrate to South Africa earlier in 1966 and returned within two weeks with horror stories backing up why I should not go there. Their comments ensured I carried out more research into the South African conditions before finally making up my mind. It was not simply a matter of packing up our bags and household items and leaving - oh no!

With my friends' concerns ringing in my ears I decided to do my own research into South Africa and its so-called troubles. I came across newspaper reports about apartheid and the problems it was bringing to all people of the country but primarily to the black population.

The major report my colleagues referred to - and which had appeared in most UK newspapers - was concerning the Sharpeville massacre. What happened in that township 50 miles (80 kms) south of Johannesburg irrevocably changed the atmosphere in South Africa. On 21 March 1960, an unarmed crowd of about 10,000 surrounded the police station, intent on burning their passes. Unnerved, the police opened fire and shot dead sixty-seven people. Pictures of the Sharpeville massacre, like no previous South African confrontation and the mass burial that followed, were beamed out of South Africa, shocking the world.

Inside the country, the African National Congress (ANC) swung into action with countrywide protests. The government was defiant and declared a State of Emergency. In the days that followed, in major co-ordinated swoops, police arrived in vast numbers, 20,000 people were arrested, and Nelson Mandela's ANC, like the Communist Party before it, was banned. ANC leaders were forced into exile or hiding and many were locked up. At the UN, the Security Council blamed the government for the shootings, with Britain and France abstaining. In South Africa the stock market collapsed and whites queued to buy guns or to apply to emigrate.

However, what the South Africa government did in 1963 was to be deadly effective. The police forces achieved a major coup in July 1963, when they arrested 17 Umkhonto leaders in a house near Johannesburg. These were members of the active military wing of the African National Congress in cooperation with the South African Communist Party in their fight against the South African government. By the end of 1964, the first phase of violent resistance was over, and for another decade the country was quiescent. Of the leaders of the ANC, Mandela and Walter Sisulu were serving life sentences on Robben Island four miles (six kms) from Cape Town. Robert Sobukwe, founding leader of the Pan Africanist Congress too, was jailed on Robben Island until 1969, when the government released him but kept him politically impotent by banning him; he lived in Kimberley until his death in 1978. I can confirm this impotency since I lived in Kimberley and surrounding districts for five years and never read or heard anything about Sobukwe.

Similarly, after Sharpeville there was a significant downturn in reports of trouble from South Africa. Research shows that after June 1964 when Mandela was sent to jail, the prisoners were soon almost forgotten by the media in Britain and America. In 1964 the Times had 58 references to Mandela, in 1965 two, in 1966 none. Within South Africa the name of Mandela was even more completely obliterated, through laws which forbade any mention of the ANC or its leaders. The activists seemed to have disappeared.

Therefore I arrived in South Africa not knowing too much about apartheid (separate freedoms) and its practice (discrimination and inequality) and on the brutality of the apartheid state - the pass laws, forced removals, house arrests, and detentions without trial, which I will cover in greater detail later. Other, (extremely strange, to us), decisions made by apartheid legislation were separate facilities for entrances to certain shops such as post offices for blacks and whites, separate beaches, toilets, buses, ambulances, hospitals, schools and universities. However, within one day of arriving in South Africa, we came up against an example of one of the laws - separate railway stations for blacks and whites, which was totally alien and ridiculous.

One other reason for the lack of knowledge regarding apartheid was the fact that South Africa did not have television. The government would not allow TV until 1976, hence the majority of news was conveyed via print and mail.

Several complimentary reports and books from Chesterfield library that I had read and that had swung my decision in favour of emigrating commented that:

"While apartheid was taking root in South Africa, political power was flowing in the opposite direction in the rest of Africa. From 1957, Britain transferred power to African nationalists in the Gold Coast (Ghana), soon to be followed by the other British territories in West Africa - Sierra Leone, Nigeria, and the Gambia.

"By that time, African nationalism had swept eastward and southward into the British territories where there were significant pockets of white settlers. Early in 1960, Prime Minister Harold Macmillan of Britain toured tropical Africa and then visited South Africa. On February 3, in the Parliament in Cape Town, he spoke of 'the wind of change' that was sweeping over the continent and made it clear that Britain would not support South Africa if it tried to resist African nationalism. Over the next four years, the British transferred power to local nationalist parties in Tanganyika (Tanzania), Uganda, Kenya, Malawi, and Northern Rhodesia (Zambia). In 1965, the white settler government of Rhodesia postponed a similar outcome by asserting sovereignty over the colony and making a unilateral declaration of independence. No country recognized Rhodesian independence."

Just before we emigrated to South Africa, Britain commenced transferring power to Africans in three other neighbours of South Africa - Basutoland (Lesotho), Bechuanaland Protectorate (Botswana), and Swaziland. Successive governments in Pretoria had tried to persuade London to allow South Africa to incorporate those three territories, as had been envisaged by the South Africa Act of 1909. But after 1961, when South Africa became a republic and left the Commonwealth, incorporation was no longer possible.

We assumed from the above that South Africa may be about to change its rigid stance towards the non-whites in their country. How wrong can you be?

One pleasing aspect on our move was going to be a vast improvement in climate, reported as follows:

When winter begins in the Northern Hemisphere, summer starts in South Africa. The South African climate is rather stable and even winter months (June to August) are comparatively warm and dry. The only exception is the Cape region that has a Mediterranean climate, meaning that it receives the largest rainfall during the winter months. The rest of the country can be summarised as being almost tropical: short afternoon showers in summer and beautiful dry and crisp winter days when snow on the Drakensberg mountain peaks is not unheard of. During the summer months, temperatures throughout South Africa soar into the 30 degrees Celsius range. Although Cape Town is very dry between October and February, it can get very humid in the Natal province which is flanked by the warm Indian Ocean.

Life is a gamble and as I was brought up in Pot Lane where gambling was an everyday occurrence, our forthcoming venture to South Africa seemed to be a very good bet to me.

In the spring of 1966, with confirmation of Anglo's offer to move to South Africa, we began preparing for our departure to South Africa. The first item was to concentrate on selling our bungalow at 9 Ivy Close, Old Whittington, Chesterfield. Having several months' leeway before leaving and being reluctant to pay handling fees to an estate agent, we elected to make our own sale arrangements. Our adverts in local newspapers and notices in our front window soon elicited an agreed sale. Fortunately, Iris's parents had already offered to make us welcome in their home. This gave us the opportunity to spend quality time together before we set off for foreign shores.

Iris notified all our friends with the news and advised them we would update them with our new address when available. Unfortunately this was to be a constant job with a number of different house addresses in the next seven years.

I knew telling our relatives we were considering upping sticks and moving to South Africa was never going to be easy. Especially in the case of our close family - parents, brothers and sisters - we knew the reaction was likely to be mixed. On the one hand, our loved ones were pleased we were making a positive move with our lives and doing something which we believed was going to bring us happiness. On the other hand, the fact we were moving such a long way off was likely to be a big wrench.

One of our friends accused me of abandoning our parents, who didn't understand the need for all this travelling. Wasn't success in England enough for me? Why change horses in midstream and leave England just when I was settled in my job as a contracts engineer? Wouldn't I end up forgotten by my friends in my own country? It was a chance I had to take.

What I didn't want to do was to put off doing something unpleasant until I absolutely had to, which is why you hear so many stories of emigrants who didn't tell their relatives they were emigrating until the week before they were due to leave. Presenting our decision to emigrate as a cut-and-dried matter in which your relative has had no say is unlikely to lead to a positive reaction. Being open about the whole process was my preference. We agreed to share our thought processes with our closest relatives and keep them updated on our progress. That way they were not left out of our decision to emigrate.

Having said that, it nearly ruined our relationship with Iris's mum and dad. They were much closer to their grandchildren than my parents and were initially devastated - primarily because we had lived with them before we had moved to our own bungalow and had always seen so much of one another while we lived in the UK. They also felt that I had hidden things from them, and that it had been a breach of trust. However, because I told them as early as I could - even before going to London for the interview - they must have felt part of the decision-making process.

The second important point was to emphasize the positives of emigrating. Instead of dwelling on how we would see one another less, I concentrated on the plus-points of living in South Africa - the opportunities that we and the children would have there. We were careful, however, not to be unrealistic. The final selling point of the whole idea was that it was only for five years.

We didn't want all the hard work we had put into our close relationships before emigrating to go to waste, so we made sure we would keep up our efforts after arrival. We told them we were going to write to them every month and if and when it was possible for them to fly to South Africa, for a holiday, any of them would be very welcome once we had settled in. Maintaining a high level of contact over this initial period turned out to be relatively easy for us since we missed them so much. Asking our relatives to visit us at an early date also eased the transition for both parties and Iris's mum and my sister Sandra joined us for a six-week holiday within 18 months of us leaving the UK.

And yet for me, who had to make the final decision using my judgement, since I was the only one who had most of the available facts, my main conclusion was based on who comes first, our parents and friends or us, the family carrying out the actions. I believed at the time that I had sufficient good reasons for emigrating, although I recognised there were a number of risks involved.

How could our parents make such a decision when their background and beginnings were so different? I don't want to go into a detailed history of our families; I will keep to a few selected facts, which may possibly help to define this most difficult and intangible dimension of our South African journey. Both of our mothers and fathers were born and bred in Derbyshire and had always stayed in Chesterfield, as did the majority of their families and ancestors going back to the early 1800s. Their knowledge of South Africa and any other foreign countries were extremely limited and they were unable to offer much criticism of what life would be like out there.

Knowing that we were going to the Orange Free State with its warm to hot and mainly dry climate we decided to buy as little in advance as possible. There wasn't much point in taking our English-style clothes with us, especially the winter ones, so we ordered no special supplies of food or medicine. I felt as if I had inside me all the medicine that I could ever need, as a result of the absurd and ever-growing number of injections against smallpox, yellow fever, diphtheria and polio. On the advice offered by Bill, doctors, and books from library and AAC we bought relatively few items to take with us to South Africa. One of the first items I bought myself after we arrived in Welkom was a safari suit, with short trousers.

One major concern was that our children, Leon and Andrew, would have a lot to leave behind when moving abroad - something they would not necessarily want to do. However, knowing their athleticism and interest in anything new, especially related to wild animals and sports, which were abundant in South Africa, we made the decision for them. I was confident they would easily cope with making new friends and the challenge of learning a new language.

Anglo provided us with an excellent map of South Africa and various booklets and magazines before we left the UK, which helped us to understand more about the country and some of the culture and way of life of whites, blacks and coloureds.

I then prepared a checklist of what needed to be done before our move. Anything we needed on our planned return in five years time was stored at our parents' houses. We involved the children, who decided what they wanted to take themselves. We offered anything we didn't want to family and friends and anything left over was donated to charity.

We had a session emptying the loft, cupboards, garage, and garden shed. Since we had several months before we left, it seemed to be ample time to do everything. We sent postcards, telling everyone who had need to know that we were leaving the country and we would contact them with our new address, to friends and family when we got there.

We obtained a leaflet from the post office about mail and contacted our bank, phone, electricity and gas companies, estate agent, doctor, dentist, passport office, Leon's school, insurance company, employer and all the 'official' people who need to be notified.

What were the assumed benefits of emigrating to South Africa?

The opportunity of meeting people from our own and other countries, as well as the locals.

A social life that would certainly be different, plus a new landscape and a far better climate.

New ways of looking at things, new discoveries to be made, especially for the children.

Learning new languages like Afrikaans, Zulu, Xhosa.

The enjoyment of meeting a challenge, and hopefully succeeding.

A more stable financial situation and an improving one once I had obtained the Engineer's Ticket which would help from the point of view of minimising stress as well as in more obvious practical ways.

For our own peace of mind, we would want enough money to be able to get home, if we needed to.

We'd be living and working for up to five years as part of a community with its own distinctive culture, so we'd be sharing skills and building lifelong friendships.

There were other advantages to consider too:

A cheaper way of life and a lower cost of living, including free or cheaper subsidised accommodation. Hence, the chance to save for our future back in the UK.

Job opportunities which I didn't have at home with my superiors well entrenched and not due to retire for a long time.

An international perspective on work and business backed up by an improved lifestyle for all the family.

Finally, the ability to travel to see a large part of Southern Africa including the wild animal parks, the capital cities such as

Johannesburg, Cape Town, Durban and Bloemfontein, and the former British colonies such as Lesotho, Botswana and Swaziland.

For my part, even though I had read about South Africa I had little idea what to expect and I could only guess what lay in store with a little apprehension. As we began our final preparations for the long flight I was a bag of excitement and nerves. There was the thrill of an epic new journey with a clear direction, beginning and end. But there was also the uncertainty of a true exploration.

There was no doubt this was going to be an adventure of a lifetime, well, five years hopefully, but with every quest there is an element of risk, and we would be facing more than we'd ever known before. What with a new job, employer, different living conditions, new schools etc it was up to me to minimise those risks wherever possible and enjoy our time in South Africa until such time as we returned to the UK.

Iris, with two young children to look after, didn't have time to research the subject of South Africa but relied heavily on my judgement. She had far less of an idea of the real Africa and it eventually evoked incredible emotions for her with the change in the landscape, the people and its history. Without the assistance of our parents and close relatives she would have to withstand as much pressure, if not more, in looking after the children in such a strange country and environment.

On a sunny but cold day in September 1966 the Thompson family said goodbye to a Britain of the Swinging Sixties and embarked upon a journey to go beyond the Equator to work and live a new life. Excitement and anticipation were tinged with apprehension because our destination, the recently created independent Republic of South Africa, was frequently the subject of international concern.

It was in this anxious mood that the journey began. Although the thrill of going to a foreign country was there, the main thought now was the next 48 hours or so and the three stops we had to contend with during our long flight to South Africa. There was no direct flight in those days from Heathrow to Johannesburg Jan Smuts airport, now renamed the Oliver Tambo airport. We were travellers condemned to dreary hours of waiting and preparation on the ground; to tiresome formalities with customs, exchange, and immigration controls at all kind of places, and finally to a cumbersome and ponderous journey by rail until we reached our destination of Welkom in the Orange Free State.

Our extended journey from Chesterfield started on Saturday morning by train, travelling to St Pancras on the LMS line. Leaving the station seemed to happen in a flash. One minute, there we were, the flutter of a handkerchief, the wave of a hand or a face looking back at us through the window and the next thing on the train to London. We left little behind us in Chesterfield - our family and some good friends but very few possessions.

We had no complaints over the speed at which we travelled to London but after reaching St Pancras the hassle began. We took the underground to the nearest station to Heathrow and finally a taxi to the airport. We flew from Heathrow to Johannesburg via Frankfurt, Luanda in Angola and Windhoek in Namibia (formerly South West Africa) which, by coincidence, had its opening day the same day we landed. The final arrival time at Johannesburg Jan Smuts Airport was early afternoon on Sunday.

Anglo had organised all of our tickets for each stage of our journey which included the train from Chesterfield, Underground, flight and the train ticket from Johannesburg to Welkom. They also arranged the times of each stage so all we had to do was to turn up at the appropriate time, sit back and try to enjoy the trip. After we arrived at the airport in South Africa they organised the transfer of us from Jan Smuts to the Johannesburg railway station, our tickets, our stop at a nearby cafe and search for nappies. When we arrived at Welkom we were to be met by an official who would escort us to a local hotel.

At the Heathrow terminal we admired the long shape of the Boeing jet crouched on the approach to the runway and as it started forward we said our goodbyes to the England we had grown to love.

The flight was with British Overseas Airways Corporation (BOAC) and not South African Airways since many countries had stopped trading economically with South Africa, and refused them the use of their airspace, which naturally affected the airline. Our extended route was 626 miles (1007 kms) north east to Frankfurt with a one hour turnaround to pick up passengers. Then it was 4,225 miles (6798 kms) south west to Luanda with a stop for refuelling, 982 miles (1580 kms) south east to Windhoek, and 735 miles (1183 kms) south east to Johannesburg. From Johannesburg to Welkom was another 140 miles (225 kms). This was a nightmare to say the least.

We fastened our seat belts and lay back in the seat of the Boeing 707, feeling slightly nauseated with relief. Nearly 6,000 miles (9654 kms) to Johannesburg, thought yours truly. In fact we covered almost 6,600 miles (10620 kms), with my stomach starting to heave. Some children began to play in the plane, just the excuse for Leon and Andrew to start exploring the aircraft. Each leg of our journey to Africa took us further away from what we knew and closer to something we could only imagine. The greater the distance we were from home, the more powerful was the urge to huddle close together and to hold tight to the one thing we were sure of, the family. So the flight was solace not hardship, with Leon and Andrew sleeping on blankets spread on the floor at our feet.

The stewards came round, took the last orders, brought out extra blankets, lowered chairs and tilted them as far back as they would go, helping passengers to settle for the night. It was by this time very dark. For a while the lights of Frankfurt and the surrounding area made a pretty pattern on the ground behind us, but they quickly disappeared. Soon there was no concentration of light anywhere below. When one's eyes had grown accustomed to the night, we became aware of the fact that down there it was all foreign land or sea.

We all felt Africa long before we saw it. Its hot breath reached out to us off the coast of Mauritania, a dusty desert wind that signalled its approach in a haze creeping over the horizon. Round about this moment it became apparent that we were not only flying over desert but also through desert air. The aircraft began to pitch and toss violently. The stewards came hurriedly to the aid of their passengers. The hostess dashed to the children. Safety-belts were quickly fastened around both waking and sleeping bodies. Lights flashed on and off. Then came the first signs of life as we descended towards the capital of Angola - Luanda.

We landed at Luanda in time for breakfast. But that same morning, only 24 hours before, we had been having our meal in England and in the autumn, whereas it was now spring in Africa or late winter. Luanda is one of the most humid places on earth. Even though it was only early in the morning I was dripping sweat from every pore of my body. Fortunately I was the only one of our family to venture into the terminal building for a look round.

Two hours after landing we were airborne again. The plane had a new supply of fuel and oil, a new crew; its inside had been cleaned, dusted, and sprayed and now smelt strongly of insecticide.

We next landed just outside the town of Windhoek as the sun came up. A native immigration officer and a native customs officer quickly passed us through the controls. We were greeted by African models offering free drinks and food to celebrate the opening of the new airport. What a welcome!

In less than an hour, rocking violently, the plane was back in the sky, in the dusty, turbulent air over the desert town. Morning tea-time, that abiding, almost fanatical ritual of Southern Africa, was observed elaborately on the plane, with trays full of fruit cakes, chocolate cakes, cream-sponge, and walnut cakes, pastries rich with cream, with jam, custards, with half a dozen varieties of sandwiches, with fresh fruit and, of course, with cups of Rooibos tea. Just after all this had been consumed, at about noon, the clouds below us were suddenly parted and Johannesburg appeared. Soon the airport was almost exactly underneath us; a long way down but unmistakable, the dumps of the gold mines in clear view. With a view like this I felt a rush of affection for South Africa but tinged with fear I had done the wrong thing. "Doors to manual", the intercom sputtered. "Welcome to Jan Smuts International Airport". I had spent a desperate night on a packed BAOC flight from London, via Frankfurt, Luanda and Windhoek with my wife and two small children.

We arrived at Jan Smuts airport, outside Johannesburg after a 22 hour flight from Heathrow on Sunday 4 September 1966. The final arrival time was early afternoon. We climbed with relief out of the plane and made our way to the arrivals section.

We were met at reception by an Anglo representative who directed us to his car drawn up under the portico of the airport and the chauffeur opened the door for us as we continued our journey into the unknown.

He drove us to the railway station in Johannesburg to get the train to Welkom. By then we had run out of Terri towelling nappies and had to search Johannesburg for a chemist to buy emergency disposable nappies for Andrew, which weren't easy to find on a Sunday afternoon.

The agent handed over the four rail tickets plus South African money for food and dropped us off for a short stay at a café for a meal and a cup of tea near the mainline railway station in Johannesburg. It was almost dark by the time we turned into the station and boarded the train for Welkom.

Doors slammed along the line of coaches, a whistle blew and the train trembled into movement. As the train set off the jerk nearly shot me out of bed but we were away. The station lamps sailed by us into darkness and we retired into our sleeping-berths. I lay awake most of the time, listening to the sound of wheels on the track and the clickety-click (clickety-clack) which is now lost back home in the UK. The train we took to Welkom must have been the milk train, stopping at every station, being shunted into sidings and going very slowly in between so as not to be in the way of the express and goods trains or waiting for some slow cross-country train. Out in the dark nothing was visible, except for the occasional flash of lights from a small station. It was still early, for the sun was low, only just emerging above the hills in the distance and we wondered if we would be seeing wild animals roaming by the tracks.

The overnight train journey culminated in our first true taste of apartheid as we initially alighted at the Welkom railway station for Africans only. Our fellow Bantu passengers were kind enough to point out the error of our ways and we quickly returned to our seats with our cases and waited for the train to travel an extra mile or so before alighting at the Whites only platform. As we finally reached our destination the train was slowing down and the impressive dark gold mine tips, reminding us of the coal tips back home in Derbyshire, rose along the line.

We finally arrived at Welkom train station at 7am on Monday 5 September 1966 to be met by Welkom Gold Mine personnel officer Oscar Stopforth. We loaded our cases and bags into his car and set off for the Dagbreek hotel, the closest one to the mine. After booking us in, he asked me to report to work at 9.00am that day, after travelling continuously since 10am Saturday. Talk about wanting their pound of flesh! Our new life in South Africa had begun.

Chapter Three

Welkom Gold Mine, OFS, S Africa: September 1966-July 1968

O UR RELENTLESS AND STRESSFUL JOURNEY lasting 48 hours had just ended. My working day was about to begin. Welcome to Welkom, so to speak.

The personnel officer Oscar gave me a lift from the hotel and dropped me off outside the resident engineer's office at the mine. I was shown into the office by a sweet old lady, a Mrs Goodwin, who turned out to be the mother of a friend-to-be, who lived in Jagersfontein. She was extremely courteous with offers of tea and biscuits to ensure I felt at ease.

At the time of my arrival at Welkom Gold Mine on this sunny, immaculate morning in September, Ron McKechnie had been resident engineer for several years. He asked me for details of my background and advised me I would be reporting to the Assistant Resident Engineer, Aubrey Taylor, and asked me to contact him if I ever wanted help with personal problems. Mrs Goodwin then directed me to Aubrey Taylor's office block about half a mile away, next to the reduction plant and the mine workshops. Aubrey advised me of my duties during the coming few weeks and introduced me to the Training Manager, George Hillhouse. George set the scene for the next three months until the end of the year and introduced me to the senior office staff and black boss-boy (team leader). In the workshops I met the Transport Foreman Jack Webster, whose father was one of the original 'Cousin Jacks', a tin miner from Cornwall who had lots of valuable expertise to offer based on his knowledge picked up from the Cornish tin mines.

Later in the week I met the Reduction Plant foreman fitter John Pinder, together with other engineering assistants. Before the end of the year, George organised for me to go to Maccauvlei for mines training, where I met a future friend Atle Grenar, a Norwegian married to Sue, a South African girl from Cape Town.

Tuesday and rest of the first week - Training on Fanakalo, a hybrid of Xhosa, Zulu and probably a smattering of other Bantu languages plus Afrikaans, English and Portuguese. This was a language used to overcome the communications barrier caused by a multitude of languages and dialects and was taught to both whites and blacks. It was a lingua franca, mainly in the gold, diamond, coal and copper mining industries in South Africa - and to a smaller extent in the Democratic Republic of the Congo, Namibia, Zambia, and Zimbabwe.

A few examples of Fanakalo, a very guttural language comparable to Scots, are:

Fika Lapa - come here

Fika wena lo shofel - bring me a shovel

Hamba Gahla - Go well

Aikona - an emphatic and irrevocable 'no'

Hamba gahle, madoda - Go in peace, man.

Indeed I became so committed to Fanakalo, I acquired the difficult clicking Bushman (Xhosa) tongue as if it were my own. This led me to adopt the unique 'Click Song' (Qongqothwane in Xhosa), sung by Miriam Makeba, as my favourite song while in South Africa. In 1966, Miriam received a Grammy Award for Best Folk Recording together with Harry Belafonte for An Evening with Belafonte & Makeba.

During the first week, after my Fanakalo training, the Bantu hostel manager invited me into one of the hostels to see some of the living conditions and appraisal schemes run by the mine. Their aim was to ensure the health and welfare of the African workers and that

26

they picked the brightest Bantu as the mine's boss-boys, a very important position, especially where health and safety underground were concerned.

First of all he showed me the acclimatisation chambers, similar to a sauna where I ran an appraising eye over the men's naked bodies and judged that this batch must be nearing the completion of their eight-day acclimatization. They were sleek and shiny, the muscle definition showing clearly through the skin. The men were then put through a series of aptitude tests which tested their usefulness. The tests were a structured systematic way of evaluating how the Bantu would perform on tasks or react to different situations. It was also part of an appraisal which regularly recorded an assessment of an employee's performance, potential and development needs.

The manager then showed me round their living quarters; long dormitories with numerous beds either side of the room in rows. He took me to the canteen to show me what sort of food they ate. The main cook was preparing 'mealie meal' in very large urns. This white maize porridge is the staple of the Bantu diet. Meat was the only food that was rationed. Each man was limited to 1lb of meat a day. The company had long ago discovered, to its astonishment and cost, that a Bantu, offered unlimited supplies of fresh meat, was quite capable of eating his own weight of it on a monthly basis. Another cook was filling a half-gallon jug with thick, gruel-like, mildly alcoholic Bantu beer, also rationed. It was educational to see how the other half lived. No wonder the mines were never short of willing Bantu workers.

At this time it may be useful to include a short history of Welkom, the black township and the Ernest Oppenheimer Hospital:

WELKOM HISTORY (extract from AAC archives)

The history of gold prospecting and mining in the Free State goes back to the late 19th century when gold was discovered and mined near Vredefort, but it took a considerable time before any substantial gold deposits were found under the open, desolate plains of the north-western Free State. In April 1948, a borehole sunk in search for water on the farm St Helena struck lava, not subterranean water. Those who inhabited the farm remained thirsty, but the lava was that of a deep-flowing source of gold ore linked to the famous Witwatersrand. Foreigners and their mines came overnight, people from the rest of the Free State, prospectors from South Africa, fortune-seekers from the world. However, at that time there were no railways, no metalled road, no electricity, no piped water - only the little farming village of Odendaalsrus.

The new Welkom was eventually established as one of the few cities in the world to have been planned to completion before so much as a brick was laid. The planning of Welkom was undertaken by Sir Ernest Oppenheimer, the then AAC Chairman, and resulted in the residential, mining and industrial areas of the city being harmoniously blended to form what was to become known as the 'Garden City.'

Mine shafts sprang up like strange flowers, their workforce establishing one of South Africa's most advanced infrastructures. A million people found their home on the Free State Goldfields, with Welkom being the principal city. When we arrived there in 1966, the Free State Goldfields were rivalled only by those of the West Rand in production and reserves.

Apart from its gold, the region encompassed several districts forming the heart of the county's maize triangle, stretching from horizon to horizon. To keep in balance with nature the region was blessed with a game reserve and two nature reserves. For flora and fauna, people were able to visit three nature reserves - Willem Pretorius Game Reserve, and the Sandveld and Soetdoring Nature Reserves. Other attractions were a great variety of bird-life to be seen on the mine evaporation dams and natural pans that surround the town. In order that this remarkable achievement could be seen in perspective, it had to be borne in mind that only 20 years previously there was nothing in the area except bare veld and mealie lands. Welkom lay in the great plain of the Orange Free State, some 170 miles (273 kms) south of Johannesburg and the Witwatersrand.

Welkom's population increased from 100 Europeans in 1947 to an estimated 35,000 in 1965. In addition, there were some 28,000 municipality domiciled Bantu in Thabong township, as well as 7,000 domestic servants living in servants' quarters in the European area. The surrounding mines employed a further 58,000 Bantu.

In addition, most of the residential suburbs or neighbourhood units had their own primary schools approached through parks or green strips. The result was the reduction to a minimum of the streets to be crossed by children attending school, and the provision of pleasant playgrounds and park-lands for each neighbourhood unit. Finally, Welkom had been so planned that there was no need for traffic lights or stop-streets; traffic flowed swiftly and smoothly. The shoppers could obtain in the town anything they were likely to need. All leading banks had branches housed in fine buildings.

THABONG

Thabong Bantu township - the name means "Place of Joy" was a model township housing some 28,000 Bantu men, women and children in homes for families, and in accommodation units for single men - all of which had water and waterborne sewerage.

The township was self-contained. It had its own post office, police station and shopping centre - the shops being owned and managed by the Bantu themselves. There were beer halls and beer gardens. There was a community hall for social gatherings, an association football stadium, all-weather tennis courts and facilities for golf and other athletics within the township itself. Thabong also had its own primary and secondary schools.

Of particular appeal at Thabong was a modern R60,000 crèche where daily 250 Bantu children, ranging from babes in arms to boys and girls of eight and nine were cared for and fed by properly-trained Bantu personnel while their mothers were at work.

The municipal health department conducted a polyclinic at Thabong where Bantu men and women could obtain free medical guidance and medicines as well as a complete inoculation service against infectious diseases.

ERNEST OPPENHEIMER HOSPITAL

The Ernest Oppenheimer Hospital for Bantu mine workers, built at a cost of R2,000,000 was the largest and most modern industrial hospital in the Southern Hemisphere. Its fame spread far and wide. It had been visited by medical personnel from all over the world, particularly as it was also a centre for research into tropical diseases.

In the newer gold mining areas, model townships have been established by the mining companies. In these townships are the houses of the mine employees as well as mine hospitals, shopping centres, hotels, churches and all the social and sporting amenities of modern life.

A feature of the accommodation provided by the mines is the availability, in some instances, of house ownership schemes. Single employees are usually accommodated on the mines in attractive hostels.

Not only has the gold mining industry set a high standard in the provision of housing for its employees, but it has also done much to provide them with sound working conditions and opportunities for leisure.

The major producing gold mines in the industry have provided swimming baths, full-sized golf courses, bowling greens and tennis courts. There are also numerous soccer, rugby and cricket fields, besides facilities for indoor games, such as snooker and darts, dancing, cinema shows and amateur theatricals.

To promote social welfare, the Chamber of Mines has established several organizations including the Social Services Department, a medical benefit society and the Witwatersrand Gold Mines Employees' Provident Fund. The industry maintains a number of hospitals.

Most of the Natives employed in the mining industry are tribal workers who come either from the reserves - large tracts of land reserved by the State for Native occupation - or from territories outside South Africa. The majority of Native mineworkers in South Africa come from outside the Union from Lesotho, Botswana and Malawi.

In their own areas, Natives are mainly pastoralists, with a low standard of subsistence. The income of an average family usually has to be supplemented by cash wages from employment outside the reserves. The South African gold mining industry offers the largest single employment outlet to the tribal Natives.

Statistics show that mine Natives go to the gold mines for seven to eight contract periods averaging about a year each. About 80 per cent of the mines' labour force is composed of Natives who voluntarily offer themselves again for employment.

Our first Saturday in South Africa, September 10, was now the time to start enjoying being there. This was the moment to revel in being different; the place to unleash our dreams. For me, the earliest evidence of our new elevated status was the acquisition of our first car in South Africa. In the UK, I had driven a second-hand Hillman Minx. Now it was a brand new VW 1300 Beetle. I didn't have much difficulty in obtaining advice from so-called friends and colleagues at the mine, who where all too willing to direct me towards a salesman who would give them a cut from the sale

We were now able to visit places of interest. The town of

Welkom had many monuments and parks such as Central Park, Peter Pan Park, Van Riebeck Park and West Park. The Ernest Oppenheimer Theatre there was named after the AAC Chairman who planned the layout of Welkom.

The small town of Odendaalsrus in Free State Province is 10 miles (16 km) north of Welkom. One of our first weekend visits was to a small farm there with examples of a number of indigenous animals including ostrich. Apart from the farmer's main stock of sheep and cattle, he bred ostriches for their low-fat meat and skin that produced fine leather.

In the first few weeks we travelled locally around Welkom hoping to see some evidence of wildlife, without success - apart from the small farm at Odendaalsrus. We then struck gold and finally saw a vista of startling beauty. Suddenly, from out of nowhere, on the outskirts of Welkom, we turned into the banks of a shallow water pan, produced from waste water from the mines, and there, before our very eyes, was a flock of hundreds of flamingos. As we got closer to this fantastic scene, seeing them in their semi-natural environment, they finally became disturbed by our presence. The startled flamingos rose from the lake, and we saw this flash of reddish pink from their bright under feathers as they set-off and flew into a large formation. At the end of one grand sweep, their red feathers blazing in sunlight, they headed north, leaving us behind with a memory never to be forgotten.

Good examples of the planning by Sir Ernest was that large numbers of trees had been planted throughout Welkom to try to cover the semi-desert conditions and unusually for a town or city of its size, it didn't have any traffic lights, which made it a car driver's dream.

Another well-planned amenity was the Welkom Gold Mine Club sports centre which offered facilities for rugby, soccer, netball, tennis, hockey, cricket, bowling and snooker - besides the all-important swimming pools; especially for the children.

Working at number two shaft for the next few weeks I was expected to travel underground with the assistant engineer or engineering foreman whose main duties were to visit the underground fitters and follow up any problems, which were affecting production, followed by visits to the major development projects.

My first time underground at Welkom Gold Mine was unforgettable. We made our way over to the changing rooms where we donned the customary white overalls, rubber boots, and helmets. This is all you wore over your underpants in South African gold mines, which are usually uncomfortably warm and humid. That, plus the bottles of water you carry with you as, dehydrated or not from the night before, you soon would be after the underground visit. I was also issued with a pneumo (short for pneumonia) jacket required to withstand the cold of travelling down the inlet air shaft, but dispensed with as soon as we reached the hot regions of the working stopes because of the high temperatures and humidity.

Off then to the shaft with the foreman fitter, Frank Cole, who I was seconded to for a few weeks, a fitter and a supporting boss-boy. Facing us was the cage which lowered miners to the depths, alternately disgorging workers from the various levels, and swallowing their shift replacements as the operation grinds on 24/7. The cage (literally a two-level cage of about 10 cubic metres) was empty apart from the four of us, as we were going down in between shift changeovers to avoid the crush. Even so, a feeling of claustrophobia crept over me, although I didn't normally suffer from the condition. A bell rang once, twice, and the floor dropped away from under us as the cage started down. My stomach came up to press against my ribs. We went down in one long continuous rush in the darkness. The cage jarred against the shaft runners with the air changing due to the heat building up rapidly with depth.

Because we were going from level one to 36 in one go, the cage operator had basically "dropped" the cage at full speed. Was this out of benevolence to save us time, I wondered? I suspected that we would have been far worse if we had been joined by the regular sweat-stained miners returning at the end of their shift. An experience I would not wish on my worst enemy.

Eventually we reached the bottom and everyone sank with bended knees as the cage operator abruptly slowed down our freefall. The onsetter opened the cage door, and as we got out of the cage I felt as though a great weight had been lifted from my shoulders as we passed through the swinging ventilation doors and tramped on up the drive towards the working stopes. The drive now was a spacious, well lit and freshly ventilated tunnel, with the vent piping, the compressed air pipe, and the electrical cable bolted securely into the hanging wall of the drive, and a set of steel railway tracks laid along the floor.

At the end of the drive, we travelled along the stopes, the underground workplace where the gold ore was extracted, checking the winches and other mechanical equipment, the pneumo jacket having been discarded because of the increase in temperature and humidity. With the change in the airways and 30 degree steps between levels my fatigue increased, as if exhaustion had produced an advanced rheumatism of its own. As a result I had to call the boss-boy back and rest for some five minutes in the airway to cool down. When my breathing became more normal, although I would have liked to rest more, I carried on my route since I had to cover a fixed area of responsibility. So despite my aching body I started on again. We travelled like this for up to two hours and fortunately didn't come across many problems that may have delayed my tour of inspection.

This was my first visit to a working goldmine, which at 4200 feet (1.28 kms) was deep by any standards, although nowhere near the East Rand mine in Johannesburg, at two miles (3.58 kms). That requires huge air conditioning machinery to keep you cool enough to work and combat the almost 100% humidity. I was not a mining engineer, but I already had a horrible feeling of what to expect with the pervading conditions.

On returning to surface via the cage I made straight for the administration building, looking forward to an ice cold glass of lime juice and water and a shower to try to get rid of the muck and stress in my body. After reporting any items that required attention I left for the hotel to check on the day's events, hopefully enjoyed by the family. This was generally not the case. Having to look after two children unable to wander outside the hotel and having to resort to playing inside on the staircases etc, Iris was forever being warned by the hotel staff of the children's behaviour and the other residents' demands for peace and quiet.

Working under these excessive conditions soon took its toll on my body. Problems with back spasms soon developed and I had to go to see a specialist who identified my problem, which had steadily got worse over the years and had mystified the doctors in Chesterfield. He discovered I had one leg three quarters of an inch longer than the other and his common-sense solution was a built-up shoe, electronic treatment and exercises to improve the strength of my back and stomach muscles which I still practice today.

Generally, after a hard day's work in the mine, it was difficult to pass the men-only bar in the hotel. I used to have a couple of bottles of lager. It now makes my mouth water just to think of it. Heavens, what nectar!

It seemed a healthy life; my appetite improved when I left the hotel. One of the major concerns of underground mining personnel was developing *Pthisis* the dreaded incurable occupational disease of the mines, caused by silica particles being drawn into the lungs and there solidifying, especially those involved in development work. This anxiety was reduced by a visit to the silicosis bureau, situated in the town, for a check up of my lungs. This was to be an annual inspection for all underground workers. Although the x-rays showed up a patch on my lungs, they said it was probably an old scar from when I had double-pneumonia as a child.

I lost two stone in weight during our six week stay at the Dagbreek hotel. This was due to the stress of the journey from the UK, the new job, being thrown into the conditions of working underground in the abnormally high temperatures and humidity. I was also unable to have breakfast because the hotel kitchen did not open until 8.30 am - two hours after I started work. This, and a series of family problems at the hotel that I had to deal with, took its toll. No wonder I suffered severe weight loss. This also had an effect on Iris, who was bearing the brunt of complaints from the children on restriction of their movements. They were not allowed by the hotel management to play on the stairs and other areas of the hotel. These were the same livewire children who were used to mainly freedom of movement in their home environment back in the UK. On the other hand the hotel manager was constantly complaining of noise etc coming from Leon and Andrew.

Initial scenes of Welkom, near the hotel, that we didn't like were the African men and a few women who were drinking solely to get drunk. They had bought Kaffir Beer and cheap wine (Lieberstein by the gallon) from the Bottle Store (Drankwinkel), across the road from the hotel and were drinking it on the pavement outside. The wine was a rough fortified wine, and they would drink a gallon of it between them with ease. These few Bantu wrecks sprawled on the grass verges, wizened men and women seeking oblivion from bottles wrapped in brown paper gave a stereotypical example of black South Africans.

After six weeks of living in the hotel with four beds in a single room, Iris threatened that if the mine didn't get us a house to move into within two days she was going home to the UK. I reported this to Oscar Stopforth and after extensive arguments with hotel and mine officials, we finally obtained agreement to transfer out of the hotel into a privately owned house (would be called a bungalow in the UK) at 16 Zomba Street within Iris's deadline.

On Monday 17 October 1966 we moved into the house near

Welkom town centre. The house, being one rented to the mines, had many good qualities. Being much closer to the centre of town than the hotel was a big improvement. This was really essential to Iris until such time as she had passed her driving test, since the hot dry climate in Welkom made it more or less impossible to walk very far.

The house was fairly large, having a lounge, three bedrooms and a kitchen-dining room, all laid out with polished wood block floors and a bathroom with shower. A major design fault was a sunken floor in the lounge. This frequently caused problems with newcomers who weren't used to stepping down when entering the room.

Externally it appeared slightly down-at-heel, surrounded by hedges, and with a corrugated iron roof that needed attention. I am sure that if Iris had picked one it would have had a great deal more charm. The back garden was virtually empty except for a grapevine, a fig tree and a wilting hedge along the perimeter. At the back of the house was a veranda, with laundry and lavatory. Built into the back wall were the servant quarters and a garage.

From the front fence to the house was the front lawn split by a pathway. This led to a large wrought iron arch, about which climbing rose trees grew. Leon and Andrew naturally used this as a climbing and swinging frame. The path finally led to a fairly large stoep (patio) covered with red clay tiles outside the front door. There was also a car's-width of lawn down the right side of the house, leading to the garage. This was called the driveway whether you had a car or not. On the other side of the house was a much narrower passage between house and fence, just wide enough to walk through.

One of the unusual aspects of the property, to us, was the vast number of ants which lived in the front garden. My friend Mike Northwood frequently used to enjoy upsetting them by poking twigs down their holes which agitated the soldier ants that came out to tackle the intrusion and withstand the attack as best they could.

The dry season was nearly over. Clear Welkom mornings

gave way to sandstorms in the afternoon when visibility dropped to no more than a few yards. The air was then thick with dust, and heavy with the approach of thunder-storms that never broke. Now, with the wind blowing from the Kalahari desert, what had been unpleasant before was almost unbearable. Although the house was supposed to be tightly sealed, the red dust seeped in to powder the furniture, the desks, the bed linen, even the interior of the refrigerator, with a thin gritty film. It settled in the hair, was sugary between the teeth and clogged the nostrils. Outside, the dust was a red glittering fog which reduced visibility to a dozen yards. When the rains started we knew what rain really was with an avalanche of it hammering the tin roof, frightening Leon and Andrew who had never heard anything like it.

The next thing to frighten us were the frequent earth tremors that occurred at any time of day or night, resulting in cutlery and crockery dancing in tune. Items skittered across the polished wooden surface of the floors; my desk itself shuddered, rustling my papers upon it. The walls of the room shook, so that the windows rattled in their frames. Tremors lasted only a few minutes and then all was still again. It was put down to settling of underground mining stopes (excavations made by the miners to get to the gold ore). Rather frightening, considering I had to continue working underground.

We made friends from people who had also turned up in Welkom to start their life on the gold mines.

These were primarily among the expatriate community, initially from introductions by Oscar Stopforth.

Mike and Zena Davies from Wales were the first couple that Oscar introduced us to. Mike was a shiftboss at WGM and rose through the ranks, especially in De Beers, where he became Divisional General Manager.

We also befriended Mike and Elaine Northwood from Lincolnshire who I met at the Dagbreek Hotel where we had stayed. To give them a break from the hotel environment I took them back home to meet Iris and the children. Iris and Elaine are still friends and talk on average twice per week after 40 years.

The meeting of Gerald Price, also from Wales, who I became very friendly with, no doubt because of all the coincidences that kept occurring and proved to be too overwhelming to be kept secret.

First of all we both went to the Silicosis Board building in Welkom for our check-ups for phthisis at the same time. Apart from the doctor, he was the only one that I spoke to, as we were leaving the building, and in the first few minutes we got on so well that I invited Gerald, his wife Pam and children to visit us at Zomba Street.

It then turned out that although he came from S Wales he had actually worked in my home town of Chesterfield; he was also a Graduate of the IMechE, same as me; they had travelled to South Africa the same week as us; he had bought Pam the same Xmas card as I had bought Iris; he had chosen some of the same furniture from the same shop in Welkom and to top it all he had same birthday as me, 8th July. Talk about synchronicity!

Then there was Barry a fitter at WGM and wife Janice who came from Cresswell, Derbyshire just a few miles away from our home town of Chesterfield. Others were their next-door neighbours Ronnie an electrician at WGM and Ann from Scotland, Harold a planning engineer and Jean from Sunderland and Chris an engineer and Judy from somewhere in South of England.

Referring to Ronnie I must say that if there's one piece of advice I would offer to a child at the outset of life, it is, don't see the New Year in with a Scotsman, based on what happened to us in Welkom. I don't know if it was the normal Hogmanay party but what happened there was that each partygoer was asked to bring a bottle of alcohol; what sort really didn't seem to matter. The party started off rather slowly since no-one was allowed to have a drink before the clock struck midnight. As soon as the chimes ended we were instructed to pour out a drink from our own bottle for every one else at the party. Every one at the party was then urged to knock back each drink poured out for them as quickly as possible with dance music blaring out in the background. What a party that was, but we all needed at least two days to recover as we walked home just before daybreak.

We were now in a permanent abode, at least for 18 months or so and our schedules were clearly defined:

My first priority was to obtain my Engineer's Ticket. The cheapest, and to me the easiest method was using the correspondence course from Veasey's College of Engineering, recommended by George Hillhouse, the training manager. The money to pay for the first set of courses had to come from the proceeds of the sale of our home in England. This had already been transferred from the Natwest Bank in Chesterfield to a sister bank in South Africa.

Iris's priorities were:

1)   Prepare Leon for school after selecting the best available, which turned out to be St Andrew's in Welkom.

2)   Furnish the house quickly; which we did over the following two weeks. The majority of our furniture was bought new from the best shop in town, Welkom Furnishers.

3)   Buy some second-hand electrical equipment like fridge and freezer etc so we didn't make too big a hole in our savings.

It was years before Iris told me how lonely and homesick she was during those first few weeks, but she didn't want to upset me. I was full of my new job, happy and optimistic about our new life, the career in the mines that had opened up for me in the space of a few weeks, so I never noticed how unhappy Iris was. Her loyal friend Elaine came over from the Dagbreek hotel on most days to cheer her up. Slowly, resiliently, Iris began to make new friends from the expatriates around us. It has always been one of her gifts to make friends, to bring people together. She built a life for herself and brought me along with her. We made many new friends over the years, notably the Northwood family, to whom we have remained very close.

Our choice of St Andrew's school proved to be a good one for Leon, surrounded mainly by English-speaking children. We were fortunate however, to have an Afrikaans family next door with small children of similar age, so their Afrikaans improved rapidly, much more quickly than mine.

In early December we commenced preparations for our first Christmas away from home. We spent quite a time buying typical African goods and making Christmas audio tapes with most of the audio from amusing contributions by Leon and Andrew. These were sent early to both families in the UK in order that they would have them by Christmas.

When Christmas arrived, with the absence of grandparents and family, we decided to splash out on major gifts for the children, Leon was seven and Andrew three. For Andrew we bought a new large pedal car which he enjoyed immensely for a matter of 12 hours. Unfortunately we left it out near the garage, just as we would have back in the UK, but when he looked for it next morning it had vanished after a single day's ownership.

Then there was Leon's bicycle. Even before his first pair of long trousers, we had bought him a scarlet 24-inch frame Raleigh to replace the three-wheeler he had loved back in the UK. The aluminium frame of the new bike was so light we called it a racing bike, especially after I had bought it with white-wall tyres and three-speed hub gears. The main problem was he was hardly able to reach the pedals even with the saddle flush with the cross bar. But, by the time of his final year at school in South Africa, the saddle was extended to its full height. I also bought an air rifle for the children and myself to go hunting with in the veld, which I still have and treasure.

These presents were bolstered by gifts received from the UK and some obtained from new friends and a Welkom Gold Mine Christmas tree event at the mine. In other words Leon and Andrew were spoilt rotten for a change which helped us all to overcome our first Xmas away from our loved ones back home.

One day Iris noticed something was missing from her jewellery bag and was so upset she reported the loss to the police. A detective was appointed to the case and he asked everyone to attend, including the housemaid, while he related the problem he had been asked to investigate - a missing watch. From that session he said he was confident the maid had stolen it but, without proof he was unable to do anything. However he assured us that there would be no other items going missing. He was confident she would keep on the straight and narrow in future, especially while she worked for us. However, it wasn't long before Iris asked her to leave since she couldn't trust her any longer.

Iris remembers just a few things about life in Welkom. She used to go with Elaine Northwood every week, wheeling the push chairs with the children in up Zomba Street, past the Dutch Reformed Church and over some rough veldt to a nice cafe where they always had strawberry shortcake washed down with apple juice and normally walked back chatting all the way with a real tipsy feeling to set themselves up for the day.

Whenever we could get a baby-sitter we used to go to the Welkom Roxy Cinema or bioscope, as it was called by South Africans. And as usual we went to the Golden Orange hotel for drinks before going into the cinema. On one occasion we saw two films Africa Addio and Dr Zhivago, which had a big impact during our stay in South Africa.

Africa Addio was an Italian documentary made in 1966 by the Italian director Gualtiero Jacopetti about the end of the colonial era in Africa. It was a violent portrait of the continent in transition; the change from white colonialism to independent black statehood.

The film was released under the names Africa Blood and Guts in the USA and Farewell Africa in the UK. The movie documented some of the disruption caused by decolonisation, such as poaching in former animal preserves and bloody revolutions, including the Zanzibar revolution, which resulted in the massacre of approximately 5,000 Arabs in 1964

Many of the scenes, however true, contained gratuitous violence. That is, the excessive violence was shown either for shock value or considered as historic archive, which caused a lot of controversy between the opposing parties.

The film had already been banned as racist in Italy and England, and the left-liberal German newspaper Der Abend described Jacopetti as a well known "racist, colonialist fascist".

Like many movies, I suspect this one had been viciously cut. The original portrayed roughly even blame for the events between the native Africans and European colonial powers. This balance was not always maintained in the cut versions, however, such as the 1970 USA release.

Plot Outline: The second official sequel to the original shockumentary, displaying cruel acts of animal poaching and violence, executions, and tribal slaughtering, all taking place on the African continent. This resulted in the wholesale massacre of thousands of people and the indiscriminate extermination of wild life. Captured on film were mercenary killer squads wiping out entire villages, executions, Mau-Mau massacres and more.

This film gained the full support of the South Africa government, suggesting their participation or involvement in propaganda of what may happen if Apartheid was removed and blacks brought to power.

David Lean's Dr Zhivago was the exact opposite, based on the novel by Boris Pasternak A story of love and romance told against the flaming background of the Russian Revolution. Zhivago, played by Omar Sharif, a poet, surgeon, husband and lover struggling for survival. What a contrast!

In addition to a luxurious cinema in the town, we used to make regular visits to the two local Sand River and the Ster wide-

43

screen drive-in cinemas to see films, especially at weekends. The drive-ins were a few miles out of town where you could watch the films from the comfort of your car. Drive-ins were like a huge car park with each row of cars driving onto a ramp facing the large screen with large vertical steel pipe stands each containing a portable speaker which you placed on your car window whilst you listened to the film score.

On one such evening, even after dark, the air was warm. The sky was ablaze with stars, and the crickets were making nearly as much of a racket as the film score was. It was a new moon and the stars were clear and bright. They were magnificent. As we turned our faces up to the constellations and we recognised some of them we wondered what was the major difference between northern and southern hemisphere for star gazing. Another visit to the drive-in and another night which was black and brilliant as ever. This time there was an exceptional exhibition in the night sky. Indeed the stars were so full and dripping with light that we could easily see numerous shooting stars over the few hours we were parked there.

In South Africa there was far less light contamination from city centres and hence a big improvement on watching the heavenly bodies compared with England.

One of our favourite resorts we visited from Welkom was the Willem Pretorious Game Reserve, which was approximately 35 miles (56 kms) south east of Welkom, just under an hour away in the car. The reserve was created when Allemanskraal, an irrigation dam fed by the Sand River, was built in 1960 to supply water to the Free State gold fields. The dam divided the 12,000-hectare park into a densely covered, hilly northern section, which provided an ideal habitat for baboons, bushbuk, kudu and duiker, and open grasslands to the south, teeming with springbok, wildebeest, blesbok, eland, impala and zebra. White rhino and buffalo moved freely through the park. On the summit of the surrounding hills the prehistoric settlement of dry-stone-walled huts and kraals belonging to the now-vanished

Leghoya people or the Taung tribe had been restored.

The main drawback to the reserve was that during our first visit a large troop of baboons descended upon us, some sitting on our car bonnet, obviously after food and making a complete nuisance of themselves. However we had been warned they could be dangerous so we just sat in the car, with windows closed until they had left us for the next possible feeding station, the car behind us. Public braai equipment was provided but we normally took sandwiches and crisps plus beer and wine and soft drinks. South Africa's sunny climate did much to encourage outdoor cooking and the braai was part of most South Africans everyday life. The braai is similar to our barbeque however a lot less sophisticated. Meat for a braai is exposed to the direct heat of the coals and, therefore, was purchased with care and grilled with skill and normally the man's job. Only the best quality meat was purchased for the braai.

During our stay in Zomba Street we employed a garden boy called Lanios, the most educated and friendly African I came across. I used to sit and chat with him outside on the floor of the back garden. He told me he was saving up to get married and needed a dowry of so many cows, goats or pigs. I told him it had cost me less than two Rand (12/6d) to get married to Iris, which brought disbelief to his face. What I didn't tell him was that it had cost me a small fortune since then.

One day I was chatting with the office boss-boy, who was from the newly independent country of Lesotho, formerly Basutoland. When I asked him how they were enjoying independence from Britain he told me how, within three months of independence, the country had constructed several miles of tarred roads whereas none had been built in approximately 100 years of British rule. I was shocked to hear this after always being told about the benefits of British rule.

I have already referred to my priority goal of obtaining my Engineers Certificate of Competency for Mines and Works. This meant studying for my certificate using the correspondence course over a minimum period of 12 months. Although my HND had covered 90% of a degree course - the exception being law - and I achieved a number of subject distinctions in the exams - the South Africa Examining Board would not allow any reduction for me in their stringent rules.

My HND had covered five of the six subjects of the examination - but a plea in an exchange of letters with the secretary of the Board, where I asked not to have to re-sit these subjects, was rejected.

Veasey's Engineering College was established in 1924 to train young engineers to study for the Government Certificate of Competency examinations. The examinations were conducted by the Department of Education on behalf of the Departments of Labour and Mines. The Certificate was colloquially known as the Ticket, and without it an engineer could not manage a workshop or mine section.

The question papers were prepared by the Commission of Examiners with members from the Department of Labour and Mines. When qualifications and experience had been accepted, students could enrol for the examinations at a technical college of their choice.

It is good to be reminded one's vision can still be the driving force towards wholly individual achievement. I was an engineer and after nine years at Chesterfield Technical College had become accustomed to passing exams. I faced the Veasey's correspondence course with initial relish, knowing all I had to do was to complete the course work and previous exam questions to be able to pass with flying colours. However it meant keeping to a tight schedule of completing the course work within two days of receiving each section and posting my results back in order to receive the next item. Multiply this by three for the different courses and I had little time left to spend with the family, especially when I was undergoing extensive stress of on the job learning underground, starting at 6.30am, with no food until I returned home at the end of the shift.

Not wanting to fail the exams I slaved over the correspondence books like a gladiator in training, but always with a sense of past achievements. After nine years of studying at college I had developed several methods of passing exams and having a semi-photographic memory certainly helped. Lots of prospective engineers, writing their ticket, took time off in lieu of holidays whereas I, a husband with two children, couldn't really afford to take a holiday.

Most of my studying was done in the evening, after work, and Iris assisted me by keeping Leon and Andrew quiet while they were indoors. My key role during that period was in the position of Underground Construction Engineer, which wasn't very exhausting apart from the six weeks I spent working underground with my bad back. Fortunately this didn't affect my exam performance. Casting my eye over the front page of the first part A examination paper, I noted several questions the same or similar to Veasey's old exam papers and relaxed completely as my memory came into play. I walked out after an hour of an exam paper supposed to last 90 minutes having checked my answers twice.

Supremely confident after the first paper I proceeded to finish the rest of part A exams in a similar fashion. However, this supreme confidence produced a void which was to be filled with despair. The mental exertions working up to and doing the ticket exam, together with the bodily stress that I had suffered, took its toll and I had to have a week off work with a nervous breakdown, less than eight months after joining Welkom Gold Mine.

Recalling my conversation with the office boss-boy, we decided that part of my rehabilitation should be a visit to the Maluti Mountains for a weekend break.

Lesotho is an enclave within South Africa. It is a mountain kingdom, sometimes described as the 'Kingdom in the Sky'.

The country achieved independence from Britain in 1966. The rugged highlands of Lesotho encompass the Drakensberg,

Maluti and Thaba-Putsoa mountains. It also has fertile river valleys, a rich variety of flora and fauna, and a strong cultural heritage, kept alive by the Basotho people.

One Friday afternoon, we and our sons set off for the Golden Gate Highlands National Park in the upper valley of the Little Caledon River and the foothills of the spectacular Maluti Mountains of Lesotho. This 11,600-hectare reserve preserves a strange landscape of brilliant yellow, orange and red sandstone cliffs, and high outcrops and caves, pummelled into bizarre shapes by water. Early hunters were driven out of this area by the Sotho, who settled on the secure heights of the sandstone outcrop 'fortresses'. The reserve has a variety of animals and birds, including black wildebeest, black eagles and blue cranes.

After weeks in the dry plains of Welkom and the OFS, it was a relief to find a road winding into hills with woodland and meadows. Suddenly the air was cooler and the grass was greener. There were streams and orchards. Cresting a rise, we saw, to the east, the awesome ramparts and pinnacles of the mountain kingdom of Lesotho reaching far along the horizon. We were heading for the foothills of the Maluti Mountains that used to be a good place for hiding stolen cattle and were now a good place for getting back to nature. The dirt road ran past fields filled with bales of honey-coloured wheat and cattle that were fat and sleek, in a land dozing contentedly in the afternoon sunshine. Arriving at our destination, we stayed in a rondavel, or circular mud hut, with walls plastered with mud and cow dung. This really was back to nature. The guest quarters were plain and simple. Each one contained rudimentary furniture - 2 beds, chairs, cupboard and table. There was a communal washroom and lavatory in the centre of a long Nissan-type hut. After our evening meal we could appreciate the beauty and stillness of the night. A full moon had risen above a sharp outline of black mountains, washing the valley with silvery light.

Next day we thoroughly enjoyed ourselves exploring the

valley around the hut. We collected samples of plants and had such a busy and interesting day that the time flew by. Returning to the rondavel after sunset, we found all our fellow guests round a fire, drinking and chatting about the day's events.

The following morning, I looked at my watch. It was six o'clock, and the first light of the day could be seen on the thorn tree outside the bedroom window. Smoke from the morning fires, that fine wood smoke that sharpened the appetite, was in the air. I could hear the sound of people on the paths that crisscrossed the bush near his house; shouts of the children on their way to school; men going sleepy-eyed to their work in the town; women calling out to one another; Lesotho was waking up and starting the day. People arose early to get involved in their labours.

The rest of our day was spent in quiet contemplation and thinking about what had been achieved in our short stay in South Africa. Staying there, right in the mountains, which proved to be the most peaceful place on earth that we had visited, helped me to overcome my illness.

On returning to work at the mine, I found the Underground Construction Engineer had completed his holiday. Once more I was back to being a plain engineering assistant with a lower status and, even more importantly, a lower salary.

At the end of my shift on Friday 19 May 1967, I turned up at the Examination Board offices to view the exam results with an air of optimism which would have done credit to Dickens' Mr Micawber. When I saw I had failed, I knew they had made a mistake. Apart from being told I had passed that afternoon by Danie, a fellow Engineering Assistant who had a friend who worked in the exam office, I knew from my similar UK exam results for the subject that no way could I have failed. It must have been a clerical error or worse.

The following day I received a letter from the Commissions of Examiners confirming I had failed two subjects. I knew this was either a serious examination board cock-up or that the secretary was showing who was boss and being extremely vindictive, spiteful, call it what you will, in view of our previous communications.

On Monday morning I went straight to see the Resident Engineer, Ron McKechnie, and poured out my soul to him. I showed him a copy of the standard exam result paper showing pass/fail next to each other and a slip of the pencil was the difference between euphoria and misery. I doubt the examining staff who designed that sheet had ever actually sat an exam in their lives and certainly never received such an abominable piece of paper related to such an important matter after so much effort had been expended.

Mr McKenzie immediately contacted someone high up in the exam organisation and advised me to carry on working as normally as I could and he would ensure we had a response by the end of the week. I received a letter on the Saturday, but only after more theatricals, this time by the postman.

On Saturday 27 May 1967 on a hot Free State morning, the whole family joined me in waiting for the daily postal delivery. Standing at the gate we experienced another unusual series of events. The postman called at our address and delivered some post but it didn't include the letter I had anticipated. We all returned to the gate to ask him if he had missed one but he had already cycled off, when, just at that moment, he turned and rode back to us bearing the missing letter which now stated that I had passed. What a relief. Even though I was only half-way to my engineer's certificate, I felt wonderful: intensely liberated, a floating, euphoric sensation and the only words I could say were "Champion". A statement I would repeat in 14 months' time at the birth of my daughter Julia in Kimberley.

For the first few days after I came out of the shock, however, nothing except Nembutal, a barbiturate drug, would keep me from enduring yet another nervous breakdown. I had already suffered one previously attempting to stop smoking, finally succeeding due mainly to psychology. I told myself I knew I wouldn't be able to stop but resolved to see how long I could last before taking my first drag.

This provided me with a cure path which lasted a few years before I took a chance and tried a cigar which didn't bring back the urge to start cigarettes again.

Having taken French and German at school, one of my key objectives since landing in South Africa was to learn to speak Afrikaans. Some of the Afrikaners I got to know in Welkom were friendly but loved to catch you out when you were learning their language. Their "kitchen Dutch" had developed into a language that lends itself to dry humour and coarse insults. One of the most imaginative derogatory terms is reserved unsurprisingly for English-speakers; Soutpiel, which means salt penis, derived from the perception that the original British settlers had one foot in Africa, the other in their homeland and their member dangling in the ocean between. They also took great delight in teaching newcomers rude words passed off as normal everyday language. One was the phrase 'Ek kan nie klar nie (I can't complain) but they told me to say 'Ek kan nie kack nie' (I can't shit), which brought forward guffaws of laughter.

I finally opted for a few lessons in Afrikaans run by a local language training company, situated in the centre of Welkom, which enabled me to communicate in the language, when necessary, for the rest of my stay.

Our first forays as a family into Welkom's city centre confirmed the view that shopping in South Africa were exhilarating excursions. It was here, taking turns to push a trolley between the aisles at the OK Bazaars department store that we began to realise just how wide was the gulf of opportunity between South Africa and the UK that we had crossed. We would dawdle in front of the deli counter, something we'd never heard of before. We'd never tasted such a wide variety of hams and salamis.

Back in England we had not been department-store people, we'd been market individuals. The way we shopped was as good an indicator as any of what South Africa meant to us. In England my mam or occasionally dad had shopped daily, either bussing to the market or going to the local shops to fetch whatever was needed for that day's meals. There was no point in stocking up on anything perishable because we didn't have a fridge to store it in.

In South Africa we began that great ritual of the rich world, the weekly shopping trip. Only those people with money, normally the whites in South Africa, had fridges and freezers to keep what they've bought fresh enough to be consumed days later.

Our first Christmas dinner in South Africa took place in Welkom, as at home in the UK, in the middle of the day. Despite the temperature being 100 deg F (38 deg C) in the shade, there was a full scale turkey dinner of very hot food, topped off with Christmas pudding covered in hot custard. Will we never learn?

My next memory was going to the monthly dances in the mine canteen after we had organised Evelyn, our house-maid, to look after Leon and Andrew.

The dances were held on Saturday night at the Welkom Mine canteen and in the men's bar the daily-paid workers from the gold mine were standing up to the counter three deep. The dance had been in progress for an hour before we got there. At tables along the veranda the South African women-folk sat primly sipping their port and lemonade or white wine and soda. Although they were admirably ignoring the absence of the men, they kept a constant and merciless vigil on the bar. Most of the wives already had the car keys safely in their handbags.

In the dining-hall, cleared of its furniture and with the floor sprinkled liberally with French chalk, was the local four-piece band, which played under the name of Solley Ward. The band was very good and loved playing Boeremusiek and the tappy country music seemed to cheer the crowd up and had them on the dance floor in no time. Without preliminaries they launched into a lively rendition of South African favourite tunes, and from the men's bar, in various stages of inebriation, answering the call to arms came the troops.

Many of them had shed their jackets, the knots of their ties had slipped, their voices were boisterous and legs were a little unsteady as they led their women onto the dance floor and immediately showed to which school of the dance they belonged. The environment reminded us of our local dance-hall, "Jimmies" (St James's Hall where we used to do our dancing), of the 1950s and we joined in, especially for the fast tunes where we could show-off our "bopping" capabilities.

As in all South African pubs at the time, the beer came in two kinds, home grown and imported. The most popular were the Lion lager, Lion ale and Castle lager brewed in South Africa by SA Breweries. The imported brands were led by Heineken and the Windhoek beer called Hansa. Most South Africa drinkers preferred it ice cold, with ice showing on the outside of the bottle. Otherwise it would be sent back to the barman.

After the dance it never occurred to me that I should not offer to take Evelyn home to the Thabong township, appended to Welkom where she lived, especially after she had babysat for us, even though it was against the apartheid laws. I wouldn't expect her to walk home when it was so late. Anyway, towards midnight I drove Evelyn home, mainly because Iris hadn't passed her driving test and wouldn't do so until two years later. She lived in the centre of the township with its inherent dangers etc. As I took her home, even though there were no street lights I could see litter strewn along the dusty sides of the main road leading into the area where people lived, huddled together in the small brick houses and shacks of the township. I dropped her off where she wanted and set off back. It wasn't a place to loiter.

During 1967 I attended a First Aid course run by the South African Red Cross Society who awarded me a Certificate for First Aid in Mining valid for three years at the end of the course.

From June to October 1967 I again took over the role of Underground Construction and Capital Foreman with responsibility for the monitoring and control of construction costs and labour on major Gold Mine underground and treatment plant projects.

Working as the UCC Foreman I had to understand all aspects of underground and treatment plant processes. The foreman fitter at No.2 shaft, Frank Cole and John Pinder, the Reduction Plant foreman and their staffs soon had me understanding the intricacies by describing and showing every part of their domain during their maintenance and installation activities. If they were too busy I accompanied individual fitters on their maintenance rounds. Also as acting Estimator I needed to obtain approximate costs of all capital items to be installed in new projects and reasonable estimates of plant and labour to install the machinery and estimate contingencies in case of unforeseen problems.

The Mining Methods explained to me were as follows:

In the Witwatersrand Series, the gold-bearing reefs occur in sheet-like deposits tilted at varying angles to the surface. Tunnels, known as cross-cuts, occur at various underground levels; usually about 100 feet (30.5 metres) apart are driven horizontally to intersect the reef. Further tunnels, known as drives, are then cut at right angles to the cross-cuts.

The drives, in turn, are connected at right angles by still further tunnels which follow the plane of the reef. Upward tunnels are known as raises; Downwards are called winzes. The areas between the raises and winzes become the stopes, where mining takes place. Pump stations, ventilation and cooling systems, underground workshops, power lines for underground locomotives, reservoirs, lighting and communications are a few of the many services which have to be provided.

On the surface is a reduction plant and mechanical and electrical workshops.

The fundamental operation of gold mining, however much some of the processes may have been mechanized, remains the drilling of holes in the rock and the blasting out of the pay reef. Over the years refinements to this practice have been introduced but it remains basically the same as it was at the start of the Witwatersrand goldfields in the 1880's.

Gold is found in the reef almost entirely in the form of very fine specks which are rarely visible. To recover it the reef has first to be crushed and ground to pulp so as to loosen the specks of gold from the surrounding rock. This part of the process is carried out in the crusher station and milling plant. The resultant product emerging from the mills is pumped to spiral or cyclone classifiers where slime and fine sand are separated by centrifugal action from coarse sand and grit before being pumped to a set of large cyclone classifiers where the slime is separated from the sand. This then passes to the cyanide plant where the gold-bearing slime is collected in large-diameter settling tanks, from which the residue is pumped into tall narrow-diameter tanks known as Browns or Pachuca tanks. Here the slime is diluted with a little extra water. The mixture is then agitated by means of compressed air. Dry cyanide (or a strong cyanide emulsion), is added to the pulp and rapidly dissolves in the water, forming a weak cyanide solution. This solution dissolves gold and silver but has no effect on the rock particles that constitute the slime. (The principle is the same as that of stirring up a mixture of sugar and sand in a cup of water; the sugar dissolves in the water while the sand remains unaffected). After the cyanide solution has dissolved the gold, the pulp is filtered through rotating canvas covered drums while the gold-bearing cyanide solution is collected in tanks. From these tanks the solution passes through a clarifying unit to a precipitation section, where the gold is precipitated from the solution by the addition of zinc dust. Zinc has the chemical property of replacing the gold in the cyanide solution, the gold precipitating from the solution in fine specks. The gold, with some surplus zinc dust and certain other impurities, is collected on canvas filter leaves in small tanks.

The gold concentrate that collects on the filter leaves is removed periodically to the smelt house, where after further treatment it is placed in crucibles for smelting in a reverberatory furnace. At high temperatures the concentrate and flux melt, or fuse, and the impurities present - largely lead and zinc oxides - combine with sand and borax to form a slag. The gold and silver are unaffected by the flux and, being much denser, remain at the bottom of the crucible under the slag. The crucibles are removed from the furnace and their molten contents poured into iron moulds. The metal is broken away from the slag when it has solidified.

The gold bullion obtained is weighed and the individual pieces, called "buttons", are grouped together in threes and fours to give a total weight of about 1,000 oz. troy. The groups are re-melted and the fused mixtures poured into brick-shaped moulds to solidify as gold bars. These are sampled by means of a hand drill and the exact proportion of gold and silver in each bar is determined by assaying. After being accurately weighed, the bars are ready for despatch to the gold mining industry's central refinery for final purification and sale.

The projects I was involved in alternately as UCC and Estimator over an 18 month period were:

The underground project at No. 2 Shaft was a twin sub-incline shaft system to provide access between the 45 and 52 levels, east of the main shaft which was started during that period and the hoist chambers were excavated for both the service and rock inclines. The cost of this sub-incline shaft system was estimated at R900,000 spread over three years. The hoist was expected to be installed and operating towards the end of the 1967 financial year.

It had also been decided during the year to split the gold slimes in the reduction plant into high-and low-grade streams to enable an upgrading of uranium to be achieved in the high-grade residues (Twin streaming). This enabled an enriched fraction to be produced from 28 per cent of the total milled slime and this material was to be deposited separately for possible future uranium recovery in 1967. There was an increase in estimated expenditure at R1,250,000 which was primarily caused by a renewed interest in uranium by the world at large (from the Welkom Gold Mine annual reports for 1966 and 1967).

On Saturday 22 July 1967, to celebrate my part A exam results and take my mind off work and problems, I went to Bloemfontein on my own to see the Springboks play rugby. The match was against France at the Free State Stadium where one of my favourite players Piet Visagie of Griqualand West made his debut for the Springboks.

It was the first international game I had ever seen but what I did know was that France would be up against, what was then and still is now, some of the hardest rugby players on the planet. These men were the type who didn't yield, not an inch, to anyone, especially when defending in their own back yard. The whole match was much more physical than I ever imagined and the domination of the SA pack was obvious from the start. However, the French put up an excellent rearguard action and managed to keep the final score down to SA 16 France 3.

Scorers were left wing Corra Dirksen N-Tvl 1 try, inside centre Eben Olivier WP 1 try, right wing Jannie Engelbrecht WP 1 try, full back HO de Villiers WP 2 conversions and Lock Tiny Naude WP 1 penalty and France: 1 penalty

I had a good view of the match but was surrounded by Afrikaans farmers, which turned out to be quite fortuitous for me, a lone 'Engelsmann'. I was extremely well received trying out my Afrikaans and every time the Springboks scored I was inundated with offers of biltong and cans of lager. A good time was had by all and I returned from the match with more biltong than I took.

It's amazing the little things which stay in your mind about occasions like that. The attendance was 46,000.

Written confirmation that I had passed in Part A of Engineers examination was finally received on a standard form on Wednesday 23 August 1967. There were unclear crossings-out and no date on the advice, another example of a bureaucracy run by incompetent, mainly Afrikaans personnel.

I was then transferred to No. 3 shaft where I was involved primarily with the engineering foreman responsible for both surface and underground activities. However, the Section Engineer, Jack Hyde, had taken an instant dislike to me. I never knew why, but it was clear from the activities he allocated to me - which were the dirtiest and most dangerous he could find. Shortly before I arrived at No. 3 shaft there had been a major fire underground and one of my first duties, instructed by Mr Hyde, was to visit the area of the fire to survey the damage for insurance recovery purposes. I was one of the first to go there after the fire, with the accompaniment of a mine captain and a shift boss.

Even though the fire had been put out weeks before my visit, the heat and devastation of equipment were still in evidence. We found ourselves in a chamber, the size of an average room, but the fire-blackened roof was only a few feet high. As I played my lamp across the hanging wall the view was wicked. The rock had cracked and was very ugly. 'A bunch of grapes' was the term. Due to the excessive heat, parts of the roof of the stope had fallen in on the winches and associated equipment and most of them had to be scrapped. If they hadn't been crushed by falls of rock their innards had been exposed to such excessive temperatures which ensured they had to be replaced.

As a result of our visit and reports, the mine made an insurance claim for loss of equipment and the engineering foreman included in it the loss of engineering tools including two sets of Swiss-made spanners and sockets, one of which was allocated to him and one to me, I suppose for compensation for my comprehensive report without protest.

Next day, I was pulled out of the stopes and put onto special development studies. Whether this was to give me other opportunities, or to show who was boss at No. 3 shaft, I am not sure but I took it on the chin and did it without complaint. What I do know is that the working conditions - noise, dust and humidity - for the miners in the development tunnels were the worst I have experienced, and the workers, both black and white, deserved all the money they received for the dangerous and extreme operating conditions. Eventually I think Mr Hyde realised he wasn't going to intimidate me by sending me to the most dangerous places and finally decided to leave me to my own resources, working with the foreman fitter.

This change of direction helped to reinvigorate me and I started to enjoy life once again. Part of this energy affected my relationship with Iris which had been under stress since we had left home. She had already given me two sons, and now we both wanted a daughter. What better token of love, mutual need and loyalty could there be than a baby? A few months later, in November 1967 we were overjoyed when Iris confirmed she was pregnant and we naturally hoped for a girl.

One of the lasting memories of Welkom mine No. 3 shaft was the Christmas party of 1967. It was given by the officers to all the manual workers and was held at the shaft on Saturday 23 December 1967. The party was well organised and the planning concentrated on drinks and food for the workers (mainly black labourers and boss-boys). Two people, I was one of them, were delegated to go to the local off-licence to purchase the spirits, beer and copious amounts of local cheap wine and visit the local market to obtain provisions for the giant soup manufacturing facility. The soup or broth was cooked in cut-down 45 gallon oil drums which were sliced in two and although some attempts were made to clean them, it was quite noticeable that during the cooking rainbow-coloured swarf developed at the top of each. All the vegetables - potatoes, cabbage, cauliflower, carrots and onions - were cut up and deposited in boiling water which had been prepared in the two oil drums and cooked for two or three hours. Additional oil drums were provided for the manufacture of a mixed cocktail of spirits - primarily cane - lots of cheap Lieberstein wine and beer all mixed together to make an extremely strong concoction. The interesting part came when the soup and drink were served to the African participants. Boss-boys lined everyone up in order and they dished out the broth, into their hard hats, and drank to each worker in their handsome mugs. The Africans didn't bother with knives and forks but tucked in with their hands. And also as was usual with the African workers they drank not so much to enjoy themselves as to get drunk. Within hours, bodies were lying all over the place from the effects of the strong alcoholic cocktail.

Our own second Christmas party in Welkom was spent at Mike and Elaine's home where Iris and Elaine cooked dinner consisting of a main course of duck, a speciality of Lincolnshire, where they had lived. Unfortunately, it turned out to be a disappointment since there was hardly any meat on it to carve. However the rest of the food and drinks were good and we were able to let our hair down as usual.

On Monday 26 February 1968 I was accepted as a candidate for the Engineering Examination in Mining Plant and Mining Law by the Board of Examiners for the final exams to be held in March. Because of my bad back I was given permission to miss a few days at work, which enabled me to knuckle down to some last-minute revision. Welkom Gold Mine management realised that with my late entry into the exams I needed a little extra support in achieving my ends - obtaining the pass for Part B of the Engineering certificate. I sat the final part of the exams and once again felt confident that I had passed with flying colours.

From March to May I was again acting as UCC Foreman for eight weeks, working on the No. 2 shaft underground projects and the Twin Streaming Capital project in the Reduction Plant.

On Thursday 16 May 1968 I was informed that I had passed South African Mechanical Engineering Cert of Competency Mines and Works examination held in March 1968 and my salary increased from R260/month to R390/month, an increase of 33% overnight. Oh what joy for me and the whole family. Passing my Govt Certificate, an essential item in South Africa prior to calling oneself an Engineer and following normal procedure, all my workmates now called me Mr Thompson. So there we were, overnight, with the change in status from an engineering assistant to a full engineer and the various class trappings that go with it. It took a little getting used to, but we managed. Having said that, a new vigour crept into everything I did, after passing my ticket.

Life is certainly full of surprises, especially mine, and within a month I was told that I was to be transferred to De Beers Mines Consolidated in Kimberley, Griqualand West, as a section engineer on their diamond mines. As a result of my success, one of the treats I bought for the family was an Alsatian dog, which we called Bruce. This was purchased from our office receptionist at the mine and whilst we were in Zomba St and Kimberley it turned out to be an excellent guard dog but was ruined when we transferred to Jagersfontein, which I will explain later.

Before we left Welkom to go to De Beers we decided to go to see the tribal dancing, with friends, at the No. 3 shaft amphitheatre. This was a site specially built for dancing where competitions between the races were held every month on a Saturday afternoon. The competitions were encouraged by the hostel managers on the mines. From the initiation of tribal dancing, dance teams and their supporters were defined and separated along ethnic lines. As many dance movements were brought from the home area, they were easily distinguishable from other tribes' dance styles. In this way, an ethnic identity was established and, as a Chamber of Mines pamphlet stated in 1947, 'competition between the tribes is encouraged.'

We all went through the main gateway and down to our reserved seats in the front row and joined a merry jostling throng, much like the crowd at a bull ring. The Master of Ceremonies called out each of the race participants in turn as we settled to watch the spectacle. They performed a dancing show - presenting different tribal dances and singing traditional songs accompanied by drums, a kudu or duiker horns and rattles and whistles. 'The Shangaans!', 'The Zulus!', 'The Basutos!', 'The Xhosas!' all took it in turns to demonstrate their capabilities.

A typical description of one of the tribal dances:

"A number of drummers appeared from the entrance, dressed in their brief loin-cloths, their long wooden drums hung on rawhide straps about their necks and they took up stations around the circular earthen stage. One of the drummers commenced the music with a beat on a big old drum, and the performance began with the barefoot dancers gyrating and stamping their feet in a python-like movement.

Silence gripped the amphitheatre as the other drummers stooped over the drums that they clasped between their knees; they began to create the rhythm of the dance. It was a broken, disturbing beat that jerked and twitched, a compelling, demanding sound, the pulse of their race. Then came the dancers, shuffling, row upon row, headdresses dipping and rustling, the animal tail kilts, swirling, war rattles at the wrists and ankles, black muscles already oiled with the sweat of excitement, coming in slowly, rank upon majestic rank, moving as though the drums were pumping life into them.

A cry from the lead dancer and a shrill blast on a kudu horn and the ranks whirled like dry leaves in a wind, they fell again into a new pattern, and through the opening in their midst came a single gigantic figure. Immediately the drums changed their rhythm. Faster, demanding, and the dancers hissed in their throats a sound like storm surf rushing up a stony beach.

The main dancer flung his arms wide, braced on legs like black marble columns, his head thrown back. He sang a single word of command, shrilling it, and in instantaneous response every right knee was brought up to the level of the chest. Half a second's pause and then all the dancers' horny bare feet stamped down simultaneously with a heavy sound on the stage that shook the amphitheatre to its foundations. The men continued to dance, and reality was gone in the moving, charging, swirling, retreating ranks."

Most of the women watching were completely lost in the erotic turmoil and barbaric splendour of it reminding them of the films Zulu and Zulu Dawn. The series of dances proved to be one of those never-to-be-forgotten experiences.

I must relate another unusual social difference between South Africa and the UK.

When I first heard African people calling others - complete strangers - their brother or their sister, it sounded odd to my ears. But after a while I knew exactly what it meant; it was a form of community spirit that I had heard before in my youth living down Pot Lane. It was generated from a mix of poverty, sincerity, humility and an absence of vanity and an enjoyable way of communicating for free to all concerned.

After 18 months of living at Zomba Street I came across a psychological aspect peculiar to Bantu. This was if you give them a special gift as a reward for good work, they will leave and not return. After this had happened three or four times I was told that the African's interpretation of it was they should have had a similar gift every week and suggested to them that we had been short-changing them in previous weeks or months.

As mentioned earlier I was surprisingly transferred from Welkom Gold Mine to De Beers Consolidated Mines Ltd Kimberley on 8 July 1968, my 30th birthday. That was to be a challenge that proved to be better for us all round, with Kimberley being designed much more on UK lines and far more English, especially in its historical development.

Chapter Four

De Beers Consolidated Mines, Kimberley,   N Cape: July 1968

K IMBERLEY HAS SO MUCH diamond history built into the 120 years since it was named that I feel it is important to mention some of those pertinent points before I continue my story in what was the centre of the world's diamond industry.

A History of Kimberley (as described in the De Beers archives)

"The place had always maintained its sparkle, an interesting city, full of character. In its early years it had been the second biggest city in South Africa and the wealthiest in the world, having its streets lit by electricity before even London and Paris. It attracted to its opera house and theatres some of the world's greatest singers and actors, staging international boxing contests, upstaging today's larger cities of Cape Town, Durban and the then newly found Johannesburg. The city built on greed and nurtured on vanity was churning out its most precious commodity, diamonds. There were still plenty of them being produced in 1968 with four mines Dutoitspan, Bultfontein, De Beers and Wesselton Mines operating; along with CDM another De Beers company were producing more diamonds than anywhere else in the world. This was the product, worthless apart from its beauty and industrial usage that slick marketing had transformed into the ultimate symbol of wealth and romance.

In its heyday, when the world's richest seams of diamonds were not only mined but marketed from here, and international prices were fixed by such young diamond magnates as Cecil Rhodes and Barney Barnato, Kimberley had called the diamond tune even over New York, Amsterdam and London, and the bustling young city had reflected this power. It seemed an unlikely spot for a city of wealth to have sprung up.

Here in semi-desert hundreds of miles from other cities, a bucket of water sometimes cost more than a bucket of whisky and, initially, the only transport links were the stagecoach and the covered wagon. The surrounding aridity made the green lawns around the mansions of the diamond magnates so striking. Sprinklers had to stay on incessantly to create those lush grass verges and flowerbeds, offsetting the wrought-iron balconies and pillared verandas of the wealthy. Because this had originally been a mining camp with its design determined by which claims yielded diamonds, much of Kimberley wasn't a pattern of squares and regular blocks as in most cities, but a hotchpotch of winding streets and odd-sized, odd-shaped properties."

The establishment of the town had started with the discovery of the first mine at Dutoitspan, quickly followed by Bultfontein.

DUTOITSPAN AND BULTFONTEIN MINES

"Since early times in the existence of the human race, individuals have pursued the dream of instant and easy wealth. Whether by alchemy or adventure, the goal has been the same.

No mere words, such as 'diamond rush', can possibly describe the reality of the frantic activity that resulted when rumours of a possible 'find' where spread about. Very rapidly an area could be transformed into a chaotic jumble of tents and wagons; an unhygienic area, littered with the detritus of human and mining activity. Amidst these chaotic scenes entrepreneurs emerged; some to organise claimholders and others, honest or otherwise, to promote schemes to attract investor/speculators in the cities. The very mention of diamonds was sufficient to tempt the gullible investor.

The first authenticated diamond discovery in the Cape Colony in 1866 had attracted some diggers to the alluvial deposits in the Vaal, Orange and Harts rivers but had been viewed sceptically by the outside world. However, later finds led to renewed interest amongst small-scale diggers.

Dutoitspan mine was the first of the Kimberley diamond mines to be discovered. The 6,000 acre Dorstfontein farm originally belonged to Abraham Paulus du Toit, who had built a small house next to a pan, a basin-shaped depression holding water. The farm was named Du Toit's Pan for obvious reasons. Eventually the farm was bought for £870 by Adriaan J van Wyk in 1869.

The first diamond was found on the farm in 1869, possibly by van Wyk or his wife, who at first did not realise the value of their find, but there are several other candidates for the honour. By late 1869 there were numerous diggers at Dutoitspan and by July 1870 a number of them were operating claims. William Alderson, later to be a shareholder in De Beers Mining Company, heard of the discoveries and he and his group pegged out their claims. Van Wyk was powerless to prevent the diggings and eventually accepted seven shillings and sixpence a week per week for each claim of thirty square feet from the diggers. Disputes arose about claims and boundaries and van Wyk was glad to dispose of his land to The London and South African Exploration Company for £2,600.

Shortly after Dutoitspan, further discoveries were made in October or November 1869 on an adjacent 14,434 acre farm, Bultfontein, owned by Cornelis du Plooy. It was reported that farmer Du Plooy discovered diamonds when plastering the walls of his humble home. But he did not know at the time they were diamonds since he thought they were merely shiny pebbles.

Diggers, chiefly Boers with their families from the neighbourhood, flooded in to Bultfontein, prospecting throughout the area and the farm became a prolific source of diamonds and a mine richer than the Dutoitspan Mine. By the beginning of December 1869 it had become quite common knowledge that a partnership of investors had paid Cornelius du Plooy £2000 for his farm.

In 1888, De Beers Consolidated Mines Limited was incorporated. Included in its portfolio was a controlling interest in the Dutoitspan and Bultfontein mines. Finally De Beers purchased them from The London and South African Exploration Company in 1899 for £1,625,000.

The largest brilliant-cut diamond discovered in modern times was the Stern Star at 223 carats which was found in 1974 at Dutoitspan."

This was followed by the founding of the third mine which was called the De Beers Mine.

THE HISTORY OF DE BEERS MINE

"The De Beers Mine was discovered in May, 1871 on the farm 'Vooruitzicht' at Griqualand West. The farm was owned by the brothers Johannes and Arnoldus De Beer who had bought it ten years previously for £50. A Richard Jackson was the first to realize that a large pipe (a large extinct volcanic pipe containing diamonds) existed on the farm. Soon after this discovery the brothers sold the farm to the Port Elizabeth firm of Dunnel, Ebden and Company for £6,000.

By 1872 the news of the discovery had spread far and wide and soon there were over 50,000 people on the diamond fields. Men from all walks of life and from all countries rushed there. In this year Cecil John Rhodes arrived on the diamond fields. The town created by this influx was known as New Rush and later Kimberley after Lord Kimberley, British Secretary for the Colonies at the time.

In their efforts to extract as many diamonds as they could, as quickly as possible, the claim holders encountered great difficulties in the jumble of holes, pits and burrows due to the collapsing of roadways between the open diggings. Each claim holder was endangering his neighbour the faster and deeper he dug. This led to the ingenious system of horse whims, horizontal wooden wheels 14 to 18 feet across, with which loads were hauled to ground level by horses or mules. The disasters of open pit workings were frequent and when the mine had reached a depth of 350 feet it became evident that only by consolidating all the holdings into one unit, was it possible to go ahead with systematic underground mining. A shaft was started in 1884. Already the first application of modern mining methods to the South African diamond fields had been made by the introduction of steam washing gear. Steam pumps were also used to overcome the influx of water as the mine became deeper. Ripple washing machines or cradles were used for the first time in the washing of the diamondiferous soil and, later, rotary washing machines.

By 1886 the mine had reached 400 feet and opencast working was discontinued because of rock-falls into the mine. Efforts were being made to protect the mine from further hazards caused by the opencast workings and the reef was cut back in terraces but this safeguard was tried too late. A year later Cecil Rhodes, in partnership with others, had succeeded in gaining sole control of the De Beers workings, thereby forming the De Beers Mining Company. With this move a system of underground mining was started.

De Beers Consolidated Mines was incorporated in 1888, having taken over assets representing the whole of the De Beers Mine and three-quarters of the Kimberley Mine. Cecil Rhodes was Chairman and Barney Barnato one of the life governors. Both a vertical and an incline shaft were sunk and the blueground, after mining, was spread out in the sun and rain to weather, making recovery simpler. There were no crushing and recovery methods as there are today. This weathered Kimberlite was then pulverized and put through a series of different mesh-sized sieves, the final residue being carefully sorted.

The then system of chambering was devised and applied by

Gardner Williams in 1889. Underground mining continued until 1908 when the De Beers mine closed down owing to the depression. The 'big hole' of De Beers Mine, 500 feet deep, had yielded 23,201,719 carats of diamonds. The amount of earth excavated from the mine was 40 million tons.

The mine was kept dry until 1942 when pumping ceased and the workings were allowed to flood. De Beers mine was dewatered between 1949 and 1953 and sampling operations carried out on the 820 ft and 1000 ft levels in order to establish the payability of the un-mined western section of the pipe. On completion of these operations the mine was again allowed to flood.

Pumping was re-started in April 1961 and was completed in 20 months. The mine was re-opened in 1963 after being dormant for 55 years."

And finally Kimberley Mine, the richest of them all (details of which appear later under the heading Kimberley Mine Museum since the mine was actually closed when I joined De Beers in 1968). I firmly believe that Kimberley has stayed the centre of the diamond world through the strength and forward-looking plans of three people; all champions in their own right and time. They were Cecil John Rhodes and Ernest and Harry Oppenheimer.

RHODES AND BARNATO

"The consolidation of the South African diamond industry owes much to the thrusting, often ruthless, enterprise of two British born entrepreneurs, Cecil Rhodes and Barney Barnato.

Cecil John Rhodes, the son of a vicar, was born in 1853 in Bishop's Stortford, Hertfordshire. The health of young Cecil was not good and, in 1870, aged 17, he was sent to Natal with the hope that he would benefit from the dry atmosphere. There he joined an older brother, Herbert, a farmer.

In 1871 he joined the rush to the Kimberley diamond fields

and established a business hiring steam-driven pumps to the diggers. Applying his profits to the purchase of claims in the De Beers mine in 1873 he soon realised that existing methods of working individual claims at greater depths would become impracticable. He began to extend his claim territory by means of partnerships with neighbouring operators.

Such was the extent of Rhodes' energy and ambition that he also found time to enter Oriel College, Oxford. He stayed for only one term, in 1873, returning later to study but had to journey back to South Africa in 1878 to concentrate on his mining interests.

Barney Barnato, originally Barnett [Barney] Isaacs, the son of a tradesman, was born in 1852 in Whitechapel in the East End of London, where life was hard. Young Barnett was a larger-than-life character who made his way in a tough environment. Working as an entertainer, he adopted the name Barney Barnato. The contrast in background and upbringing between Rhodes and Barnato could scarcely have been greater.

News of the Kimberley diamond rush encouraged Barnato to follow other family members to the Cape Colony in 1873. Despite having only modest means he began to deal in diamonds, eventually acquiring sufficient funds to purchase claims in the Kimberley mine. By 1880 his accumulation of successful claims was sufficient for him to consolidate his holdings at the Kimberley mine into the Barnato Diamond Mining Company.

In 1876 legal restraints on the number of claims an individual digger might own were lifted, allowing syndicates to form. This enabled Rhodes and his partners to combine their claims in the De Beers mine to form De Beers Mining Company Limited. By 1882 the 3600 individual claim holdings of 1878 at the Kimberley mine had been consolidated into 50 syndicate holdings. By 1885 the number of individual claims at the Kimberley and De Beers mines was dwindling fast, absorbed by syndicates and larger companies. Only a handful of major players was left, of whom the principals were Cecil

Rhodes and Barney Barnato. In the following years Rhodes's company aggressively bought out claims at the De Beer mine so that by 1887 it owned every claim.

Mining in deeper ground required methods beyond the means of individual diggers. The introduction of steam engines had created boom conditions. With these changes productivity increased dramatically. Rhodes recognised the need for the regulation of distribution because total world production of diamonds was such that prices on the international market began to fall.

After making huge profits from speculation Barnato agreed in March 1888 to give up his shareholding in Kimberley mine in exchange for gaining the largest shareholding in a new company, De Beers Consolidated Mines Limited. The company's assets were considerable. It owned the whole of the De Beer's mine, three-fifths of the shares in the Kimberley mine and a controlling interest in both Bultfontein and Dutoitspan. Barnato had 7,000 shares in the new company; Rhodes, 4,000. Subsequently De Beers acquired the remaining shareholdings in Dutoitspan and Bultfontein mines and bought the newly discovered Wesselton mine.

After relinquishing his interests in De Beers, Barnato became involved in gold shares during the final decade of the century. However, he became disillusioned with the political situation in South Africa. During his return voyage to Britain in 1897 he fell from the ship and drowned.

By 1889 Rhodes had achieved a complete monopoly of all Kimberley's mines - 90 per cent of the world's production. Together with the world's principal diamond merchants, he then set out to achieve a marketing monopoly of the diamond trade to ensure that the market could be manipulated to the best advantage, keeping supply in line with the highest price available. He established the London Diamond Syndicate, based in London, the main trading centre for rough diamonds for the previous two centuries.

Rhodes had been interested in politics in the Cape since 1880.

He represented Barkly in the Cape Assembly and became Prime Minister in 1890, resigning in 1895. Within the United Kingdom he was a member of the Privy Council and also a supporter of the Liberal Party. He gave generous financial assistance to the cause of Irish Home Rule. Rhodes had a grand vision. He believed in the pre-eminence of the Anglo-Saxon race and the British Empire as a force for good.

His policy in southern Africa was to secure the extension of British territory and he became managing director of The British South Africa Company, whose territory became known as Rhodesia. He was active during the Boer War (1899-1902), being involved in the defence of Kimberley during the siege of that town by the Boers.

Rhodes suffered from ill-health throughout his life. He died in March 1902, aged 48, in Cape Colony and is buried in Zimbabwe. He was unmarried. His will provided for the establishment of scholarships at Oxford for Americans, Germans and members of the British Empire/Commonwealth via his Rhodes Trust. His last words were said to be, 'So little done, so much to do.' Through this Trust the work that he would have done has continued."

Examples of this are Bill Clinton, former President of the USA, who obtained a Rhodes Scholarship in 1968 to attend Oxford University for two years and the Mandela Rhodes Foundation which was announced in February 2002 when the Rhodes Trust, as part of its centenary celebrations, entered into a partnership with the Nelson Mandela Foundation and made an initial donation of £10 million (R142 million) to the foundation.

ERNEST AND HARRY OPPENHEIMER

"Ernest Oppenheimer was born on 22 May 1880 in Friedburg, Germany. Aged 16, he joined a firm of diamond merchants in Hatton Garden as a trainee diamond valuer. He displayed such expertise within the business that by the time he was 21 he was sent to

Kimberley as a buyer for the company.

Although, during his first fifteen years in South Africa he was chiefly occupied in buying diamonds, he became involved in the development of gold mining on the East Rand, and built his financial base in gold. In 1917, using British and American financial backing, he formed Anglo American Corporation of South Africa (AAC) to mine gold in Southern Africa. One of his first moves in 1919 was to buy the South West African diamond concessions held by German companies before the war. A year later Oppenheimer, soon to be knighted for raising a regiment during the Great War, formed Consolidated Diamond Mines of South West Africa (CDM) to acquire and consolidate these assets. Diamonds had been found in Angola in 1912 and Oppenheimer was able, in 1923, to gain a contract to purchase the production. In 1918, in the Belgian Congo, the world's largest industrial diamond deposits - alluvial and pipe - had been discovered. AAC joined the Syndicate in 1924 and, the same year, Oppenheimer advised at the AGM that, in his experience, only by limiting the quantity of diamonds put on the market, in accordance with the demand, and by selling through one channel, could stability of the diamond trade be maintained. He was elected MP for Kimberley in 1924 as a member of the South African Party under General Jan Smuts. Two years later he was elected to the board of De Beers, becoming Chairman in 1929.

The years after the 1914-1918 war saw chronic instability in the diamond market due to over-supply. The danger to the security of the diamond industry, as Sir Ernest said some years later, was not the discovery of a new rich diamond field, but the irrational exploitation of it. An efficient mechanism that would bring together the output of new producers with those of De Beers to regulate sales had to wait until Sir Ernest was in a position to take command.

In 1925 he formed a second diamond sales syndicate that soon eclipsed the old one set up by Rhodes. Five years later he founded the Central Selling Organisation (CSO) that, before long, was regulating the sale of about 80 per cent of the world's production of uncut diamonds. Therefore Sir Ernest accomplished on an international scale what Cecil Rhodes had accomplished on a local scale. Following a crisis in the industry between 1929 and 1930 he obtained the agreement of the producing concerns outside the control of De Beers to market their diamonds through a single channel. The Central Selling Organisation had developed its skills above all to maintain both stability in the diamond trade and confidence in diamonds as jewels of beauty and lasting value. Stability was necessary for the well-being of the industry, not because production was excessive or demand was falling, but simply because wide fluctuations in prices would destroy public confidence in a luxury item such as a gem diamond. Consumer confidence would be shaken, even lost, if prices were allowed to fluctuate wildly. It was, therefore, a basic principle of the CSO never to lower its selling prices, and its chief function was to sustain and protect them. They reconciled supply and demand and when demand was stronger they had an inventory from which to add to the supply, and would at the same time increase prices; when demand was weak to curtail supply.

Realising that disposing of huge quantities of industrial diamonds (boart) might become a daunting problem, Sir Ernest formed the Diamond Development Company in 1934 in London, to develop new uses for industrial diamonds and conduct research into the manufacture of tools. Stimulated by World War Two, the demand for high-precision grinding of hard materials placed diamonds among the strategic minerals and gave a powerful fillip to their use in industry. Within a year of the war ending, Sir Ernest separated industrial diamond sales from the activities of the CSO and established Industrial Distributors (1946) Ltd to market industrial diamonds more aggressively worldwide.

During the years that Sir Ernest was creating the CSO structure, however, the diamond industry was experiencing the full impact of the Depression. Although De Beers closed all its mines, and outside producers cut down production, Dicorp built up large stocks, which it was still holding when World War Two broke out. After the war it was able to sell them for a windfall profit of £40,000,000 half of which went to the newly formed DBIT, which invested substantially in the new goldfields in the OFS and on the Far West Rand, and half to recapitalize the CSO.

Sir Ernest Oppenheimer died in 1957. During his 28 years of leadership of AAC and DBCM he had seen enormous changes at the mines but progress and success were not lost with his death. He was succeeded as chairman of both De Beers and Anglo American by his son Harry, to whom he had left his entire fortune.

Harry Oppenheimer, 49, had been active in the business since the age of 23. In the late thirties he had ruffled a few conservative feathers in the CSO by launching, of all things, a generic consumer advertising campaign to promote the sale of diamond jewellery in the United States. In 1958, De Beers entered into a partnership with the government of Tanzania to mine diamonds from the Williamson mine. The joint venture between De Beers and Tanzania was called Williamson Diamonds Limited (as referred to in Chapter 1). In 1969, De Beers formed its joint venture with the government of Botswana to form the mining company Debswana. Botswana was then the largest producer of diamonds in the world, in terms of both volume and value.

It was a remarkable achievement of the Oppenheimers that they were able to engender trust in De Beers and create a management structure of people who, although not family, were treated in this highly personal business as if they were. A quite remarkable degree of loyalty to the family, on the part of both employees and clients, cements the whole organization." Nicky Oppenheimer is the present chairman of De Beers and has continued the good work done by his father Harry and grandfather Ernest.

So on 8 July, my 30th birthday, I was transferred from Welkom Gold Mine to De Beers Consolidated Mines Ltd Kimberley, one of the best birthday presents I could have received. Although we had enjoyed our time in Welkom there had been some stressful times, which I preferred not to remember. Welkom still had that Afrikaaner pioneering feel about it and Kimberley, with its English history, seemed much more amenable to us as a family. Unbeknown to me our stay would only be for a matter of a few months, until our baby was born and considered old enough to travel to our new place of work.

When we arrived in Kimberley in 1968, 80 years after Cecil Rhodes founded De Beers, the company remained what it immediately became at its inception: the undisputed leader of the world diamond industry.

The journey from Welkom to Kimberley was one of those you want to forget since it was a very tiresome journey, especially for Iris being pregnant, and me not sure of the best way to get to our destination. I had chosen the most direct route via Boshof, with stops to look at the Salt Pans which littered the area between Bultfontein and Boshof, I took the minor road that swung west across a plateau of red dust and bush and low hills for almost 100 miles to Kimberley. We had a car full with the four of us and Bruce the Alsatian dog. A friend at the mine had said, "Drive carefully, there are lots of accidents out there. Stop if you get tired." His advice was good, but there was nowhere to stop without being broiled by the sun. I was becoming drowsy, and the road had begun to shimmer and dance in an odd manner when Kimberley appeared on the horizon. Its high buildings rose from the flat, desolate country like the vision of another world.

Leon and Andrew had been very naughty in the back seat and I finally had to stop the car, take them both out of the back and hit them hard with my hand around their legs and bottom. This was the last time I ever raised my hand to them and the memory still lingers. They were good and quiet for the rest of the trip.

As we passed through the outskirts of the town there were

disturbing landscapes where our horizon was ringed by jagged grey mountains and, overhead, the steel cables where tubs of waste travelled slowly across miles of country. This constantly fed the ever-growing mountains of ground from the mines, still containing a small percentage of diamonds which had been missed by the grease tables, x-ray machines or other lapses in the treatment plant process. However, all wasn't lost since most tips were to be re-treated using the latest recovery techniques and secondary treatment is still continuing to this day.

Our first port of call was at our new home in Ernestville (named after Sir Ernest), approximately a mile out of town. To get to the house we had to cross the main railway line running parallel with the main road from Kimberley to Bloemfontein. This was less than half a mile from the southern extremities of the De Beers mine. Leon and Andrew used to visit regularly to peer down into the enormous hole dug mainly by hand for the first 20 years of its life, producing far more gemstones, larger than 100 carats, than any other Kimberley mine. We lived next door to the Wesselton Mine plant foreman, Hennie Viljoen, who I was to work with from November 1970 when I became resident engineer at Wesselton.

My first day at work was spent at the De Beers head office in Stockdale Street, and my meeting with Personnel Manager, Vic Pearce, who introduced me to Chief Engineer, Owen Parnell, and most of his staff.

Within days Vic had introduced us to all the people we needed to know, including all the engineering families who lived near us in Ernestville. Our major contact was to be Jim Burgess, his wife Moira and children Elaine and Kim who were similar ages to Leon and Andrew. At that time Jim was Engineer in charge of the Bultfontein and Dutoitspan mines and they organised a welcoming party for us with a braai and drinks - all very civilised.

Our arrival at Kimberley was recorded in the De Beers News of the Mines as:

"July 1968 - Appointment of Sectional Engineer - Mr. Leonard Thompson

Mr L. Thompson has been transferred to Kimberley from the Welkom Gold Mine and has assumed duty as a sectional engineer. Born in Chesterfield, England, in 1938, he received his education at Chesterfield Technical College, subsequently gaining the Higher National Diploma in mechanical engineering. He is also a graduate of the London Institute of Mechanical Engineers. He was awarded the Government Mines and Works Certificate as a mechanical engineer earlier this year.

Mr Thompson commenced his engineering career as an apprentice in England and, before migrating to South Africa to take up an engineering appointment with Welkom Gold Mine in 1966, was experienced as site engineer, planning engineer and contracts engineer with various British engineering concerns. Mrs Thompson was prior to her marriage Miss Iris Stone and there are two children, Leon, aged seven, and Andrew, aged three. We are pleased to welcome the Thompson family to Ernestville and many will look forward to meeting Len on the golf course."

I don't know where they got the bit about golf from; I never had the time or the inclination.

Our De Beers welcome was topped off by an invitation to dinner later in the week at Vic's home, in the best part of town, where he provided us with an excellent meal, joined by Jim and Moira Burgess.

The following week I was given a short introduction to underground mining at the Dutoitspan/Bultfontein mine by Jim, who also introduced me to Hubert Wright, the De Beers Assistant General Manager (AGM), who was making an underground visit at the time.

It was then that I realised that within De Beers, as is so often the case with minorities, there was a preponderance of English-speaking professionals in the top echelons of the company. This was quite different to the personnel structure at Welkom Gold Mine where the majority, especially the mining section, were Afrikaans. On reflection though, the top engineering people there were English speaking.

During our first month in Kimberley we visited the Kimberley Mine Museum which was the second most popular tourist centre, after the Kruger National Park.

KIMBERLEY MINE MUSEUM

"Kimberley was the place where diamonds were found. The Big Hole is a huge pit, almost circular, mined to a depth of about 2625 feet with a surface area of 42 acres and surrounded by the city to which it gave birth. By 1914, 22.5 million tons of earth had been excavated, yielding 2.7 tons of diamonds. It is often called the world's deepest man-made hole but, for the sake of accuracy, the biggest hand-dug hole is Jagersfontein Mine, where I was due to begin work within a few months. Some modern mines, created with enormous machines, are even larger.

The techniques of underground diamond mining were pioneered at Kimberley. The mine revealed to geologists, for the first time, that the primary deposits of diamonds were ancient volcanic pipes where they had been created under extreme temperatures and pressures. Until Kimberley yielded its secrets, prospectors assumed that diamonds were found only in rivers. After the great Diamond Rush of 1871, Kimberley became the world's largest producer. This wealth ushered in South Africa's Industrial Revolution.

The Big Hole is surrounded by buildings from the heyday of the mine and the main one is now the Kimberley Mine Museum. Consisting of original and carefully reconstructed buildings, this open-air museum has preserved a great deal of the city's past. The Mining Museum enables visitors to experience 19th century mining conditions. The first officially recorded diamond discovered in the country, the Eureka, is on view there.

On a visit we wandered around the open-air exhibits. Amongst them was a small village showing the history of diamond mining at Kimberley. This complete little diamond-rush town had shops and houses; one being a prefabricated construction imported from England in 1877. There was a church, a delightful old pub, the Digger's Rest tavern and Cecil Rhodes's grand railway carriage, housing a rich collection of articles and information from the early days of the city. Beside the carriage was Barney Barnato's Boxing Academy, and on a wall was the framed original cheque signed by Cecil Rhodes and Barney Barnato for £4.5 million to establish the De Beers Consolidated Mines Limited. This was, in 1888, the largest cheque ever written up to that time.

Although the name Kimberley, the capital of the Northern Cape, evokes images of glamour and romance, the diamond heyday was an era of blood, sweat and tears, high stakes and ruthless power struggles. But Kimberley wasn't just about its big hole; we loved to take walks through the historical city centre and visit the museums, monuments and art galleries that grace some of the old Victorian homes.

Kimberley became the first town in the southern hemisphere to install electric street lighting on 2nd September 1882. The city also housed South Africa's first stock exchange.

The rising importance of Kimberley led to one of the earliest South African and International Exhibitions to be staged there in 1892. It was opened by Sir Henry Loch, the then Governor of the Cape of Good Hope on the 8th of September. Amongst many exhibits were works of art, paintings from the collection of Queen Victoria and mining machinery and implements.

South Africa's first school of mines was opened in Kimberley in 1896 before being relocated to Johannesburg to become the core of the University of the Witwatersrand, incorporated in 1922.

On 14 October 1899, Kimberley was besieged at the beginning of the Boer War. The British forces trying to relieve the town suffered heavy losses before the siege was lifted on 15 February 1900. The war continued until May 1902. By that time, the British had built a concentration camp at Kimberley to house Boer women and children. Many prisoners died through disease and other sufferings. This certainly was a black period for the British military and went some way towards good Afrikaans friends turning into people who no longer wanted our friendship; as you will see when we transferred to Finsch Mine, a few years later.

In 1913, South Africa's first flying school opened at Kimberley and started training the pilots of the South African Aviation Corps, later the South African Air Force."

Kimberley had a rich history of sport. In 1965, Karen Muir became the youngest person to break a world record in any sport. This age group record stands to this day. She set it in August 1965 at the junior world champions in Blackpool, England, in the 110 yards backstroke at the age of 12. Kimberley has also contributed to much of cricket's history, having supplied several international players. There was Nipper Nicholson, the South African wicketkeeper, who worked at De Beers and, in more recent times, Pat Symcox, the South African all-round cricketer. He was the son of my best friend, Rodger, who lived in Kimberley and provided me with excellent coaching for my bowls as well as his friendship. The first international rugby test was played at the Kimberley Athletic Club ground, known as the KAC. In cycling there was Joe Billet, who we used to watch at the De Beers Cycling Stadium on Friday nights showing his prowess as an international sprint cyclist. Elsie McDonald was a Springbok lawn green bowler.

Another weekend, for a change of scenery, we visited Scotsman's Pool, approximately 20 miles from Kimberley, to see the sights and do some fishing with a rod and line. Leon and Andrew sat down by the pool and wriggled their bare toes into the sand, surrounding the water. I baited the hook for them and watched Leon from a distance on top of a large boulder as he lobbed it into the bottomless (so we were told) green water A slight current drifted his float in a wide circle under the far bank as they watched it solemnly. Within five minutes of the first cast Leon caught a lovely yellowfish (talk about beginner's luck). Instead of hitting the rod to a 90 degrees position and reeling it in by hand, Leon, with the help of Andrew, ran up the bank pulling the fish along the floor until I arrived to remove the hook. What a thrill for them in their first fishing expedition. To top the day off we had the pleasure of seeing a live pig swimming at the Modder River weir located just prior to the pool.

We then visited the Magersfontein Battlefield, less than a mile away, situated 20 miles from Kimberley, on the Modder River road. History of the battle tells us that on 11 December, 1899, in an effort to break the siege of Kimberley, a troop of 12,500 British soldiers led by Lord Methuen, attacked a well-entrenched Boer force of 8,200 under General Cronje. The battle lasted ten days, leaving 239 Britons and 87 Boers dead. It was one of the worst British defeats in the Anglo-Boer War. A small museum at the battlefield contained uniforms, weapons, documents and photos.

It wasn't long before we were made aware of the imminent arrival of our latest addition to the family since I had to rush Iris into hospital. It turned out to be a false alarm. However, it wasn't long before Julia was born in the Kimberley hospital, three weeks earlier than planned, weighing only four and a half pounds. She had to stay in hospital until she had gained more weight and we could take her home. On the day of Julia's birth when I was told we had a little baby girl I again rushed to hospital to be told that she was so small she had to be kept in an incubator. Soon afterwards the nurse came into the room with a little bundle. She unwrapped it and there was Julia: a perfectly normal, beautiful baby girl, all I could utter was 'champion' and she has been my champion ever since.

She was the image of her brother Leon, apart from size of course. We had planned to call her Julie but at the last minute we discovered that good friends of ours in the UK had called their daughter Julie so we changed her name to Julia.

Resulting from the birth, our sending parcels to UK and receiving parcels from home increased dramatically. We also had news that Iris's mum, and my sister Sandra, were planning to visit to see us and our new arrival within the next two months.

The first thing we decided was to upgrade our car from a four-seater Volkswagen to something that could seat six plus room for a baby a cot and pram. We finally decided on a Ford 17M, available in Kimberley from a local dealer in part exchange for my VW Beetle. All I claim for the VW is that it worked for us at the time. In a modest and unassuming way, not very rapidly, but steadily and reliably, it took us from A to B with little or no problems. This particular car, a 1300cc rear-engined model, carried us a good many thousand miles over the roads of South Africa, during the time that we had it.

The superiority of the Ford 17M, built for the home market by Ford of Germany, continued the Taunus family line of saloons. The 17M we bought came as a five-door estate type and we opted for the 1699cc V4, which towered over the Beetle 10 H.P. which, with a full-load was only too painfully apparent. On the Drakensberg mountains, on our way to our holidays in Durban and Ballito Bay, the 17M proved its worth with 4 adults and 3 children on board, easily able to cope with the hills and dales.

Iris finally brought Julia home to Ernestville, to me, 6 year old Leon and 3 year old Andrew. It was another blessing, another consolation for the baby we had lost in England, the same week as my accident with the mobile crane. It was a constant joy to Iris and me how close she was to her brothers, and they to her. Even now, although they don't phone each other every day but are available for each other when they get into trouble and always remember each others birthdays etc., (although the cards are normally late in delivery.) We did something right. Julia was not an attention-seeking little girl, nor very adventurous. She grew up to be the quietest and most introverted of the Thompson clan, and her shyness got her into little trouble.

When Julia was just six weeks old I was told that I was to be transferred to Jagersfontein Mine, the first of the De Beers Mines to be discovered, in 1870, just months before Dutoitspan was found. De Beers certainly didn't allow grass to grow under this engineer's feet. Yet more movement in the garage where some of our wooden boxes, delivered to us from the UK, and now used for removals, had still not been emptied.

Chapter Five

Jagersfontein Mine, Orange Free State: September 1968

T O GIVE YOU SOME IDEA of what we were committing ourselves to when joining Jagersfontein Mine I must relate some of the history of Jagersfontein.

A HISTORY OF JAGERSFONTEIN (extracts from *The Queen of Diamonds* by Bill Le Barrow - 1969)

"Jagersfontein is in the Fauresmith district of the Orange Free State, roughly in the centre of South Africa, 65 miles south west of Bloemfontein and about 80 miles east of Kimberley. The nearest seaports are East London and Port Elizabeth, both over 350 miles away. Cape Town is over 600 miles distant.

In the flat savannah terrain of the Free State the area is an extensive conclave of the Great Karroo formation which, in past ages, was a gigantic lake in which, through untold millennia, sediment settled. This eventually hardened to form the wide, fossil-bearing shales and sandstones, believed to have once been 6,730 feet thick which covers most of the interior of South Africa. Volcanic action penetrated this mass with innumerable dykes of igneous rock, such as dolerite. Widely-scattered outcrops of this hard rock cover and protect from erosion mounds of decomposing sandstone to form the ranges of hills and isolated koppies peculiar to the area. This dolerite affords them greater resistance to the ravages of wind and water which have already swept away over 2000 feet from the former land level. In the final stage of decomposition the sandstone becomes the thin layer of topsoil which supports the hardy flora and characterises the Karroo system, famed for its stock ranches.

In the long process of wearing down the mass of sandstone, erosion has uncovered vertical upthrusts, through thick black shale layers, of volcanic breccia containing olivine, mica, enstatite, ilmenite and, of most importance, valuable diamonds. When decomposed, the hard breccia becomes the familiar diamondiferous 'blue ground' of today, known as 'stuff' by the diggers of old. Long ago, erosion uncovered one of these volcanic pipes at Jagersfontein.

The mine had a chequered career from its initial opening in 1871 and on the occasion of the mine's reopening in 1949, Sir Ernest Oppenheimer declared that the Jagersfontein Mine was renowned for the quality of its diamonds, being of exceptionally good colour and size.

An old donga (gully made by soil erosion) courses down to the power station dam. It is the most significant topographical and historical feature in the area. On its upper reaches old trees group about a perennial spring - the 'fontein' - which slaked the thirsts of lion and leopard, quagga, buffalo, giraffe and other game, long since vanished, like the Bushmen who once lived by its waters. This watercourse was the cause of the start of the mine bearing its name for, in the lower length of its sluit, the first diamond was found. This bountiful spring is, in fact, the modest genesis of Jagersfontein.

The present town originated at an outspan near a fontein where a hotel served coach passengers. A trading store, a few houses and, later, a church, formed a settlement which gradually developed into an orderly township, as were the beginnings of many platteland towns. Had there been no diamonds there would have been no need for Jagersfontein, for only seven miles westward was Fauresmith, which had served the settlers since 1848. Among the camps of the diggers and the first rude houses of the early mining companies which mushroomed in the vicinity of the open mine, the town of

Jagersfontein was preconceived, planned and built to serve the industry. Jagersfontein town has fulfilled its purpose worthily. It shared the trials and triumphs with the mine

In the early days of Jagersfontein Irish immigrants kept the place in a continuous and hilarious uproar with pranks and practical jokes alternating with free-for-all fights, especially on paydays. A resident at the time said, 'On the whole they were gentlemanly'. Jagersfontein also had its share of the shiftless ne'er-do-wells, who plagued the diamond fields in those years.

The New Jagersfontein Mining and Exploration Company, a consortium of smaller mining companies individually lacking the resources to overcome difficulties in the early years, came to the end of its tether in the 1930s. To survive it joined the great De Beers group, even though depressed conditions kept the mine dormant for seventeen years. The town had no such alternative. Without its main source of income it had to exist during those lean years on the meagre trade of drought-stricken farmers in the district and the few of the skeleton crew maintaining the mine. It staggered and reeled, but did not collapse completely and become a ghost town.

Jagersfontein was the fifteenth town in the Orange Free State, so it may be regarded old historically on its own account. Considering the area and some other small platteland dorps (rural villages) it is relatively 'pretty', as several writers have described it. It remains a grid of eight streets running east to west crossed at right angles by seven others with two extensions joining small 'suburbs' snuggled in valleys of the Northern hills. One is Newtown; the other with larger and of more opulent houses facing two roads known as East and West Kloof, still retains an air of being the fashionable residential area.

The busiest part, and life centre, is the spacious market square designed to accommodate oxwagons in convoys when these supplied the mine and town with all necessities in the old days before the railways came. On the upper Western portion of the square a dignified town hall, seating 500, seems disproportionately large. The municipal offices are adjacent. Behind them is the now moribund but once flourishing marketplace where the bell in the metal tower sounds the curfew of the day. Of recent years a children's playground and a public garden cover the rest of the square, now lined with ornamental trees and bordered by tarred streets. These are welcome improvements.

Old shops and businesses in varying conditions of repair face the square. Some have been altered and modernised. Most are much as they always were. Several retain the elevated stoeps built to transfer goods from carts and wagons, so there are no pavements. None was visualised when the square was planned.

About the rest of the town, in streets widened at the sacrifice of shady trees and small front gardens to accommodate the motorcar, conditions of the houses are similar to the shops. Most are of brick and were built at the turn of the 19th century when architects considered the extremes of climate and designed houses with walls high and wide and with steep pitched, lofty roofs. Some of the better-kept ones have preserved the fretted woodwork in the form of scroll decorations on the verandas A few still have the once common but now rare and much admired white ceilings of metal pressed in attractive patterns. Others have been cleverly modernised. The less fortunate are neglected relics.

The old school is hidden behind a cluster of new classrooms, a large assembly hall and a hostel. Next to the police station a modern hospital stands in the field where the Seaforth Highlanders camped during the Anglo-Boer War. On the side of Monument Hill the old Cottage Hospital still functions, now filled to capacity with Bantu patients. Below the highest hill the stately Dutch Reformed Church, built in 1881 and surely the best architecture in Jagersfontein, still rears its graceful steeple high above the town. Behind it a new and larger church hall replaces the old. On that site is the new building of the Magistrates' Offices and Court. Next door, and sharing a common boundary, is one of the oldest landmarks in the town, the Roman Catholic Church.

Some distance beyond Newtown, in a wooded dell, graves are shaded by serene cypresses in the peace of the village cemetery. In the deepest shade upon a broken plinth a large statue of Christ, neglected and forgotten, looks down in pity from a weathered Cross.

Farther along the base of now stark hills where vanished Bushmen once hunted and cattle of long gone Griquas grazed, the African location houses a Bantu population of mixed tribal origins. Probably the first of these were Hottentot, Tembu, Fingo and Xhosa farm labourers of the first settlers, with whom refugees of the Basuto wars sought protection. Labour requirements of the mine attracted some of other tribes such as Bechuanas and Basutos.

On the plain about a mile to the South West, beside the road to the railway station, is the village of Charlesville. Planned in the shape of a diamond it comprises houses painted in varying pastel shades and of uniform design facing tree-lined roads and avenues. Lawns, gardens, all-weather tennis courts and children's playgrounds adjoin the premises of the Recreation Club, centre of the mining community's social life. A little removed from the dwellings is a splendid grassed sports field, reputed to be the best in the district.

The first air fatality in Africa occurred here, and the greatest horse race meeting of its time in the whole of Southern Africa was run on the Jagersfontein course. The Masonic Lodge, consecrated in 1884, is the oldest in the Free State as the first one, the 'Unie' in Bloemfontein, went into recess for some years. The golf club is also one of the oldest in the Province. Last century a rugby team from this small mining town defeated a Transvaal Provincial side, and its cricket, tennis, and later, aquatic sports teams were often victorious and generally respected throughout the area, including the capital city of Bloemfontein. It was once the largest town in the Free State, second only to the capital, and was possibly the most prosperous small town in South Africa. The water conservation scheme known as

The Woolwash was one of the first and largest in the Province, and was widely acclaimed and admired.

Celebrities and famous people have visited or been associated with Jagersfontein. HRH the Prince of Wales, later King Edward VIII, spent three days here in 1925. While stationed at Philipolis, before his fame as an African explorer, Dr David Livingstone very likely preached and practised medicine in the area before the town existed."

My appointment was assistant resident engineer at Jagersfontein Mine under resident engineer Dick Gore. I was mainly responsible for all equipment underground and related equipment on the surface such as steam hoists, large boiler systems, condensers, compressors, pumps etc

During my early engineering experience at college and as an apprentice fitter I had developed a passion for anything to do with British engineering and mechanical craft skills of days gone by. My heroes were the great engineers of the Victorian age such as George and Robert Stephenson and Isambard Kingdom Brunel.

This affection embraced the architecture and machinery of Britain's once great manufacturing empire. You can well imagine my surprise and delight to find a truly great monster of a machine as I walked into the engine house and saw the Rock Hoist for the first time. Although, as a fitter. I had worked on the assembly and installation of electric mining hoists in England, this steam-driven engine was the largest machine I had ever seen. It was a true world beater. The machine had been built in Blackburn, England, and shipped out to Kimberley in about 1899 during the golden age of mechanical engineering when Britain led the world. It was a Yates and Thom Winding Engine, 31in. and 47in. diameter cylinders by 5ft stroke - single drum 12ft diameter by 12ft. wide, Originally installed at No. 1 Shaft of the De Beers Mine, it was altered from a single drum hoist to a Whiting hoist in about 1909, but had never hoisted a load as the mine had been shut down in 1908. However, De Beers Mine management gave it a new lease of life by transferring it to Jagersfontein in 1910.

At the time of its installation at Jagers it was the fastest steam winding-engine in the country, developing 2,500 horse power (HP) and was never surpassed in that respect by any other. In that year, the mine broke the world record for hoisting ore, and was reputed to have hauled 1,000 tons of ore an hour continuously for eight hours from the 900ft level (900ft below ground). It is questionable whether this record has ever been bettered. It was also the only steam winding-engine to serve any mine for so many years. This machine had hoisted almost 50 million tons of ore with only one major breakdown. This was in 1954 when the crankshaft fractured. Next door to it was the Man Hoist which developed 1,000 HP.

As part of my engineer's responsibility, I used to make a monthly tour of the underground workings to inspect all important equipment, hoists, pumps, fans etc even on higher levels where little or no production took place. On the top levels the tunnels were mainly deserted apart from the spirits of miners from years gone by. On the lower levels there was the phenomenon of a well-run mine, where, in a tour through the workings one encountered so few human beings. Mile after mile of haulage and drive was silent and devoid of life, and yet there were hundreds of men down there. This was a bit scary when touring on my own as I didn't always have a shift boss to join me but I would never shirk my duties.

During my tour I would also inspect a 5ft diameter inspection hole on the 1,160ft level where they could measure the movement of the diamond bearing ground within the perimeter of the pipe which measured approximately a mile at the top. It was extremely impressive to watch this Kimberlite, thousands of tons of ore, moving down as ground was withdrawn from below, like toothpaste being expelled from a tube - one of nature's natural phenomena.

Before being transferred to Jagers I was offered the chance to travel to the mine for a day to meet some of the engineering staff and look the place over. As we entered the town we stopped at the Jagersfontein hotel, fairly close to Mine Square where we were to live. An old building, in the colonial style, with a veranda/balcony surrounding the whole of the first floor, it was a well-kept place providing an excellent lunch time meal and demonstrated the friendliness of some of the local people. Unfortunately the hotel burnt down, and although arson was suspected, nothing was ever proven.

The house we moved into at 8, Mine Square, Jagersfontein, was probably 70 years old. A single-storey building with three bedrooms and an old corrugated iron roof, like most houses in the area. Nothing special, apart from the fleas that lived in the small bedroom at the front of the house. This was the first time I had actually seen fleas. I could see them jumping about when I walked into the room. Apparently that room was the home of the dog of the previous occupant, an ideal carrier for the unwanted residents. When this was shown to the Resident Engineer he arranged for the house to be fumigated as soon as we were able to leave for a minimum of one week. In the bathroom was an old steel bath, but no shower, which I preferred. The kitchen, next to the bathroom, was dominated by an old Yorkshire range, like an Aga, which was a boon in the winter but stiflingly hot when cooking in the summer. This forced us to buy an electric cooker during the first month as our young baby wanted her meals far more quickly than the time it took to light the coal/wood fired cooker.

All windows of the house and back porch had mesh windows and mesh panels to stop mosquitoes entering our domain. The house was surrounded by gardens although small compared to the house we had left in Kimberley. One unusual feature, for us, was a peach tree and a grape vine in the back garden. There were also two out-houses at the side of the back garden for use by a servant and for storage purposes. Large mounds of old blue-ground ran along the boundary at the rear of our houses, blocking any view of the mine. Although the probability was that any diamonds waiting to be found would only be of a small size, advances in the recovery process later on, ensured that the treatment of the ground would be profitable.

When I met Paul Du Toit on my first day he said: 'We're going to shoot some bok for the annual cull this weekend Do you want to come?' After a few seconds I declined the invitation and so I missed out on my first hunting trip due partly to ignorance but mainly because of the surprise at being asked to accompany regular shooters on their annual cull. Anyway, I didn't miss out on what they were hunting since my engineer's status earned me part of the cull the next day. I was the surprised recipient of a whole springbok and a half of blesbok. These were cut into venison portions and strips of muscle, especially either side of the animals' spines, for biltong by our newly-employed garden boy. That's where our family's love of biltong started. However, it was a bit of a shock for Iris when we returned from shopping for her to find the dead animals left in our back porch lying in eddies of their own blood. . I walked away from the outhouse as my garden boy began to dissect the two dead animals. It was natural; no different from a farmer, or my dad, preparing rabbits for the pot, but I didn't want to see it that way. I regarded them with immense sadness, confronted with the reality of wild animals being killed and butchered. I was accustomed to buying meat in sanitised supermarket packaging.

However, I was informed by Eddie Green, the surveyor, that the number of Springbok and Blesbok which were culled annually was set by Dr Rudi Bigalke, the Professor of Zoology at Stellenbosch University. He came around to all the De Beers farms on an annual basis to do a count. With this information and the grazing area of the farm the carrying capacity was arrived at and in this way the number to be culled was decided on his recommendation. I can accept the deaths of those creatures much more readily now.

No sooner had we settled in our new abode than we had to

start planning for a six-weeks' visit from my sister Sandra and my mother-in-law (Mum) which was to include showing them as much of South Africa as we could.

Early in September we eagerly went to pick up our visitors, Mum and Sandra, at the then Jan Smuts airport at Johannesburg. We took them to see friends who had moved from Welkom Gold Mine to Witbank Coal mine. This was a grave mistake since it made our journey, a round trip for us, of approximately 700 miles in a single day. We only had time for a cup of tea and a sandwich, plus a change and drink for Julia before we were back on the road, hoping to get back to Jagersfontein before it was dark. The main reason was that I loved driving my new car and assumed everyone else would feel the same.

The long trip back to Jagersfontein, from memory, was quite uneventful for most of the way. Everyone was exhausted by the drive and for, Mum and Sandra, the flight also. It was dark when we arrived at Bloemfontein with another 70 miles to go. We carried on, only to stop for petrol, a quick snack and make another bottle of milk for Julia. The rest of the trip back home was mainly dirt road. With the time nearing midnight, apart from the hum of the engine and the jolting of the car on the dirt track, there was nothing to hear or see.

Suddenly the car stopped without warning. With no lights, no moon nor traffic, at that time of night an eerie silence descended upon the scene. As you can imagine Mum and Sandra, especially being in South Africa for less than 24 hours, were naturally scared stiff by thoughts of lions or other wild animals appearing at any moment.

Well, what could I do? The first thing was to find a torch and open the Ford 17M bonnet for the first time since I had bought it to look over the engine and find out what the problem was. The nearest garage was at home in Jagersfontein, 30 miles away. Within minutes, with the aid of the torch, I had found the reason for our dilemma. A missing split pin from the accelerator linkage, which had worked loose. The pin disappeared, no doubt due to the state of the road. What a predicament! How could we solve the problem? This is where my engineering experience as a fitter came into play. The answer lay with my sister Sandra. She had long hair and used hair grips to keep it in place. With the aid of one of her grips I reassembled the connection between accelerator and engine and the car worked first time and we made it back home safe and sound. What a relief for all concerned.

As soon as Mum had settled in she started taking over the cooking duties, especially the preparation of the children's peanut butter sandwiches, Andrew's favourite, to give Iris a well-earned break.

One of our treasured possessions from that time is a sound tape recording taken at Jagersfontein. This mainly consisted of Leon and Andrew telling us about their latest discoveries in life but also contributions from Mum and Sandra about what they thought of various aspects of life in South Africa.

Iris's Mum remembers the highlights of her visit during September and October 1968. One of her biggest thrills was when she was invited to go underground with the acting mine manager to see the mining activities "at the coal-face", as my father-in-law would have said, being a coal miner working underground. However, the first thing she was shown was a view of the big hole from a small viewing platform at the top of the rim of the yawning excavation. This gave her an idea of the enormity of the operation that had started nearly 100 years before.

She then remembers going down the mine after being given a white smock to cover her own clothes and equipped with a lamp and white helmet for safety. She didn't enjoy the experience of dropping down at an unimaginable speed into the depths encapsulated in the noisy cage, shaking and rattling as it plummeted about half a mile in three minutes, and was very relieved when they slowed down on reaching the 2500 ft level to disembark.

This was an emotional time for anyone inexperienced, ranging from anxiety to panic but she relished the challenge. At the bottom she emerged into a surprisingly large, light, and well-ventilated chamber with broad tunnels branching from it.

She spoke to two people at shaft bottom who welcomed her and the next stop was for a cup of tea to help her to catch her breath. She and her guides then walked up to a higher level until she was short of breath due to lack of oxygen. She then saw Bantu workers drilling holes in rocks preparing for shot firing which she heard go off five to six minutes after leaving the area. What a marvellous introduction to the mining scene underground - a never-to-be-forgotten experience. What a story to tell her grandchildren!

At the end of the journey she returned to the surface and had a shower to remove the grime and smell of the underground activities. However, that wasn't the end of her tour of the mine since, after another cup of tea, she was accompanied by the hostel manager who showed her round the Bantu dormitories with two long rows of beds, one left and one right of rooms in their main sleeping quarters. She was also shown the vegetable gardens where they grew their own produce to supplement the mine's resources, with any spare produce going to the township. She also took great delight in talking to the two pet peacocks which graced the manager's garden.

On another occasion Mum and Sandra started walking to Jagersfontein railway station, near the African village, but were stopped by Mr Giel Meyer, the foreman carpenter. He said they must return to the Mine Square unless they were accompanied by a man since it would be unsafe the nearer they got to the township. He suggested they get into his 'Bakkie', an open top vehicle, which they did, and he returned them to the Mine Square. They felt they were treated just like school children, since he was very stern.

One morning they went next door to Doreen Parker's, for coffee. She told mum that if she had her time to come over again she would not have accompanied husband Clive to South Africa. She disagreed with the way that blacks were treated. She said she believed the blacks, given the training, would be clever instead of lazy, but hadn't had the chances offered to white men who, naturally, had used their brains. She was also very homesick for her family in the UK.

Iris always enjoyed doing her bit for the Bantu when asked. She assisted other officials' wives, under the tutelage of Maud Gore, the Resident Engineer's wife, to prepare and implement a feeding scheme for the pre-school children in the township. A thick nourishing soup was made by the men at the hostel three times a week and a roster was drawn up with two ladies on duty on Mondays, Wednesdays and Fridays. The ladies would spread peanut butter on brown bread at the Club in the Mine Square and collect the soup at the mine gate. This was all then taken to a church in the township where extra helpers would join in and serve the soup and bread. The children were always courteous to the helpers and they all used to sit in a circle while they were fed. The parents of some of the children would always thank them for their contributions and for being there to help in keeping hunger at bay.

After their good deed at the end of each week Maud would give a tea party in the afternoon for all the helpers who were rewarded with tea or coffee and lovely cream cakes.

Mum also remembers going to a local farm, where a lady doctor lived, and seeing sheep being sheared, creating a very strong smell. This was offset, to a certain extent, by a variety of coloured trees in blossom. During the visit Mum and Sandra were given thick home-made biscuits, like rusks, for dunking in their tea. They were returned to our house in the lady's Land Rover. She was very nice and well-educated, according to Mum.

During their stay with us we invited friends round for a buffet meal. Mum told me later that she was asked by the assistant mine manager to take a small parcel, containing a small box with a diamond in it, to his mother who lived in the UK. He said he would pay her well and would bring her the address next time he came to visit. Mum declined to deliver it, not knowing the repercussions if she was caught. She was right to refuse to do so considering the severe sentences that could be imposed if it had been classified as an illegal transaction.

Getting to know Clive and Doreen next door proved highly beneficial. They offered their holiday bungalow in Ballito Bay just north of Umhlanga Rocks, Durban, for us to stay while Mum and Sandra were on their holiday. This was to be more like the holidays we had at home by the sea.

Initially we took the road north to Bloemfontein, the dirt road where we had the breakdown. The land started out flattish with numerous small koppies (hills) but soon we were speeding between distant hills as we approached the wide plains before the Drakensberg mountains, the highest in South Africa. The mountains rose to form a solid wall of craggy rock that spanned the horizon. They are known as uKhahlamba in Zulu, or 'barrier of spears'. They lead us further north in our approach to Natal, in the east of South Africa, and our final destination of Durban and Ballito Bay on the coast. In the 1960s Ballito was just one of many small quiet coastal resorts to the north of Durban. Like many other families, there was every reason to enjoy a seaside holiday there with so many nearby resorts to see and enjoy.

As soon as we arrived at our holiday home Sandra removed the mattress from the bed in her room, took off all the sheets and gave them a good shake. She kept the light on all night, scared stiff of the small lizards, geckos and creepy crawlies that were about. There were also monkeys in the nearby trees and, no doubt, snakes in the undergrowth for us all to be frightened about. As far as other creepy crawlies are concerned; in Jagers, button spiders were fairly common and glow worms could be seen at night from time to time. Tortoises and "Bloukop Koggelmanne" a blue headed type lizard were also quite common. Plus there were lots of meercats and dassies, superficially resembling a guinea pig, with short ears and tail.

Ballito Bay turned out to be a perfect resort for a peaceful beach break and a taste of the sea, with numerous rocks and pools to keep us all interested for most of the time. I preferred the rocks off the bay where I could fish for most of the day. I managed to catch one big enough to eat. When I tried to cut and gut it we couldn't find a knife in the cutlery drawer sharp enough.

One day we visited Umhlanga Rocks, a suburb of Durban and a trendy holiday resort, just south of Ballito. The main attractions of Umhlanga were that it was neither as dangerous nor as sleazy as the beachfront in Durban and, during the off-season, considerably less crowded. The principal reason for safety was that, in 1962, it became the first beach to erect shark nets to protect bathers. This followed a series of attacks along the whole coast in December 1957. Umhlanga was also ideal for surfing and, with a narrow inlet, easier to keep our eyes on our two Tarzans.

Leon and Andrew were their normal uninhibited selves. When they were swimming at Umhlanga Mum kept shouting at them not to go past the shark nets. Although Andrew couldn't swim he was fearless when on his lilo and used to speed in to shore on top of the waves, whereas Leon was quite a good swimmer at his age of seven and swam like a dolphin.

We also took the opportunity to visit Durban's 'Golden Mile', the Marine Parade just down the road, at dawn. Before the crowds and humidity set in we had the wide promenade, sandy beaches and crashing waves to ourselves except for a few early rising surf fanatics and muscular lifeguards.

We had breakfast at one of the small cafés where surfers congregated to swap their wave stories. Durban's draw, as a self-contained destination with great beaches and lots to see and do, appealed to anyone wanting a seaside holiday, as long as they were white. During that time of apartheid in the 1960s, the extensive beach was split according to colour. Black people were permitted to walk the length of the whole beach but, on the whites-only Addington Beach, they were not allowed to sit down or go into the sea.

We explored the Indian shopping district off Grey Street, an exotic, cross-cultural, shopping experience, where the tangy aroma of eastern spices mingled with colourful fabrics, trinkets and jewellery in the courtyard bazaars. We also enjoyed the African shopping experience at Victoria Market, where curios and souvenirs could be haggled over and famous Durban dishes sampled at one of the traditional food stalls.

My individual preference was to have a couple of cold Castle lagers, and watch the sun go down on the small harbour. The highlight for Sandra was a rickshaw ride with Leon along the promenade, the rickshaw being pulled by a huge Zulu dressed up for the occasion in all his native finery. She still treasures the souvenir photograph that was taken. One downside to the holiday was baby Julia being quite poorly there at 13 weeks old, and Mum, with her usual commonsense, fed her cold boiled water, which helped to reduce the fever.

Returning home we took the road through the Valley of 1000 Hills, an easy 20 mile drive from Durban. This road meandered through the villages of Botha's Hill, Drummond, Monteseel and Inchanga before turning west for Ladysmith via Pietermaritzburg. When we finally got home we had to live with all doors and windows open for a few days to allow the chemical fumes and smells from the fumigation to disappear. At least it had got rid of the fleas and Sandra and Mum could sleep a little more soundly.

One of the more unusual visits was to Fauresmith, a town just six miles away from Jagers. The unusual part was discovering that the main railway line ran through the centre of the main street in the town. The only accident we ever heard of was that the train ran over a chicken, unfortunately with fatal results. The children in the lower classes at Jagersfontein school went for their annual outing on the train to Fauresmith and a picnic was enjoyed by all. The parents assisted with transport to the station at Jagersfontein and collected the children at Fauresmith station to return to Jagersfontein by car

Mum remembers Leon being a mischievous little boy, referring to him putting a lizard in the deep freeze and a small lizard in the fridge and also saying "I am going to be naughty today, I am going to turn all the furniture upside down, Gran". She also spotted Leon and Andrew peering over a railway bridge and dragged them back away from danger. Leon up to his normal tricks hid an ashtray but was told to put it back before Dad got back home and he did as he was told. Leon then climbed onto the roof and asked, "Grandma, how can I get down?" She replied, "You've got to be like a boy scout and slide down," which he did.

Andrew hardly ever wore shoes when he went out to play and loved to climb up the door jamb and then drop onto Grandma with arms outspread.

Julia was frequently poorly and was often taken to the doctor who prescribed the relative medicine. It was sometime later before we found out the main reason for her being ill so much of the time. A malformed kidney was causing infections.

Julia was just three months old when Mum and Sandra left to return to the UK in October 1968. We took them to Bloemfontein airport and gave them a tearful farewell.

After Mum and Sandra left we had to start planning what to do next. With Christmas coming I finally decided that I would like to buy a surprise present for Iris, either for Christmas or, preferably, our wedding anniversary on Boxing Day. This was to be a real diamond from De Beers that would say thank you for all she had been through in the previous two years and as a reward for accompanying me on a journey I knew she would rather not have taken. Who else would have put up with the upheaval of leaving home in the UK, travelling all that way and facing such an uncertain future in a strange land, initially not knowing anyone, bringing up our two and now three children?

My way was to contact our new-found friend, Personnel Manager Vic Pearce, in Kimberley to ask for his advice. At the time Vic was one of the few that I could trust in choosing such an important gift for Iris. He replied that if I could travel to Kimberley he would organise a meeting with a diamond dealer who would be able to satisfy my needs. I arranged to meet him at Consolidated Buildings near Head Office the following day.

The person I met was KR Eden, a Licensed Diamond dealer, who was able to tell me all about diamonds and what to look for in making my choice. He advised that the value of an individual stone was dependent on several factors, such as size, shape, colour and absence or presence of flaws.

Firstly, size. A stone of about one carat could be worth £100. Ten similar stones will be worth £1,000. However, a ten-carat stone may be worth as much as £15,000. Therefore the price per carat rose sharply as the total weight of the stone increased.

Secondly, colour. The dealer laid out a sheet of clean white paper and placed the diamond on it, bottom upwards. The aim was to compare the colour it "draws" from white paper in good natural light. Their top standard is blue-white. This was a stone so white as to appear slightly blue. Then there are stones which "draw" a yellowish tinge which they call "Cape" in different shades, then finally stones which "draw" a brown colour, which will reduce the value of a stone by up to eighty per cent.

Then they consider the stone's perfection. The ones that are flawless are issued with a certificate of flawlessness so that there can be no misrepresentation.

The dealer held up a stone between his thumb and forefinger.

The cut or shape of a stone was the fourth and final decider in its value. The shape should conform closely to the "ideal". Some stones are cut to exclude a flaw and, consequently may be badly proportioned, heavy and out of round. Experts would prefer to see a graceful stone which includes a slight imperfection rather than an unattractive, unbalanced one. He put the diamond down on the desk.

He advised that the asking price by a jeweller for that stone of a carat in size could be £200, which would be fair and correct for a gem. However, he said the colour was poor and although it was flawless it was an unstylish design. Its true value should be about £100 (R200). After his explanation of what to look for I finally chose a 0.91 carat brilliant cut diamond costing R200, accompanied by a signed valuation certificate. Iris still wears that diamond today.

What was also important to me was the thought that this gift, which was up to then the most expensive personal gift I had given Iris, was a gift from the very soil of Africa. The thought that the diamond I had chosen would probably have come from one of De Beers own diamond mines added to the significance of the gift. I was giving, to the woman whom I loved and admired more than any other; a tiny speck of the very land on which we walked. It was a special speck of course: a fragment of rock that had been burned to a fine point of brightness all those years ago. Then somebody had dug it out of the earth in South Africa, polished it and brought it down to Kimberley, ready to set it in gold. This was the least I could do to show my appreciation to Iris, especially for the delivery of my daughter Julia. I presented it to Iris on our wedding anniversary, 26 December 1968.

During the time that we lived in Jagers we visited our old friends Mike and Elaine Northwood and daughter Louise who had moved from Welkom GM to live and work at Harmony Gold Mine. The main memory was of Iris being extremely sick, suffering from gastro-enteritis after eating fish. Fortunately she was the only one to go down with it but we both spent a sleepless night with a constant going to and from the toilet.

Iris eventually started playing tennis at Jagers, twice a week for the exercise and company, plus a change from constantly having the children. It was then that we decided Iris needed to learn how to drive to give her more independence and I started to teach her in our

Ford 17M. With so many dirt roads around Jagers I got the head of security to lend me the key to the airfield which was used fairly infrequently except by the herd of springbok and blesbok. The tarred strip in the centre of the airfield proved ideal for Iris with the small hangar providing a good place to learn to reverse into. After six months of training she was ready for her driving test.

Early in 1969 I decided to start joining in the sports on offer at Jagersfontein and finished up trying four out of the multitude played there. These were golf, cricket, bowls and, finally, yachting.

Jagersfontein had a boulder-ridden golf course, a scrubby nine-hole affair a couple of miles out of town. I only tried it twice before calling it a day because my golf balls kept finding the numerous boulders - which meant extensive searching. I lost most of them. I decided it would be easier and cheaper to try something else. Eddie Green remembers the boulders on the course of which his nine iron still bears the scars. At the time, he was involved with the Mine Captain, Andrew Young, and they blasted as many rocks on the course as they could, to reduce the obstacles, but that still didn't prove attractive to me.

Since I had been elected to the cricket committee, it was only natural to show my support by participating whenever my job allowed me to do so, although I hadn't played cricket since leaving school. According to the De Beers Magazine, I did fairly well supporting our two star players, Len Drury, our Secretary and a Griqualand West cricketer and Archie Miller, my underground electrician. This was especially when playing against Koffyfontein where I was 2nd highest scorer, with 10. When we played at Springfontein I excelled with my bowling. When given a chance in the 2nd innings I returned figures of 5 for 18 (as reported in the News from the Mines - 'This time it was the spin and guile of Len Thompson that did the damage'. Unfortunately for cricket I started playing bowls, which I finally settled on as my main sport.

The main person to blame for this was Ben 'Sarge' Erasmus,

an excellent bowler, the best in the club. He took me under his wing and taught me all he knew. He also gave me my first set of composite Dunlop woods which I used for two years until I felt I needed a better set. I found that the sport suited me, I was good at it, with Ben's help and I found the bowling crowd much more friendly and sociable than with any of the other sports I had participated in. So started a long honeymoon with the game of bowls which I still play today.

The final choice of sport to try out was yachting, where I came up against Clive Parker's crazy capsizes. If I had read the December 1966 Reef magazine provided by AAC at Welkom I would have found out that next door neighbour Clive was an expert in capsizing his craft. It was reported that, as Commodore of the Spurwing Yacht Club, he had represented Jagers at the Allemanskraal regatta, where he had demonstrated a couple of capsizes for the viewing public. It should have made me wary of his offers of assistance to a naïve sailor like myself. I went to the Jagers Woolwash dam to try my hand at sailing and Clive was kind enough to offer to show me how it was done. With no demonstration whatsoever he told me to get into the yacht. I was fully dressed, and as I did so he gave it a quick push and over we went. You can imagine my surprise, and the laughter from the bank. Here I was dripping wet, my money in my back pocket etc soaked and yet another landlubber who wouldn't try yachting again.

However, I spent the rest of what proved to be an enjoyable day looking over the wide waters of the dam, where the skiers in particular relished the long runs. These outings had been instigated by Mrs. Myrna Griffiths, aided and abetted by her husband Tony, a crack skier. Tony put a lot of time and effort into coaching beginners where his helpful nature and patience enabled many to become competent water skiers. This was typical of the De Beers management hierarchy in building up the feeling of family loyalty within the company. There were also plenty of anglers catching fish such as carp and yellow fish. Alec (Pop) Sutherland had the biggest catch when he caught a 19 lb. carp. A few months later, it was reported that Ivan Brookes, the hostel manager, caught the biggest freshwater fish in his life, a 24 pounder. He dejectedly returned it to the water, for it was the spawning season for yellow fish!

To make up for my Woolwash christening incident Clive phoned me one morning and asked if I would like to see a large diamond of over 200 carats. When I went to see it I was surprised that Clive kept it in his office safe in a dirty old jam jar. It was the largest diamond I had ever seen and I asked him if he would mind bringing it to my home so that I could arrange a photograph by the mine scribe and photographer, Bill Le Barrow. Clive brought the diamond round to my house later that day and Bill took the photo which is shown on the front cover. Bill certainly knew his photography, evidenced by the picture as shown on the front cover of this book. He it was who placed the Lion matchbox behind the stone to show its comparative size. As Bill released the shutter, the harsh glare of the flash was captured within the crystal - captured, repeated, magnified and thrown back at us as we observed the creation of the small flash of yellow lightning. It was this photo that gave us the idea for the title of my book.

Later in the holiday season, we made another trip to the seaside on the Natal coast, this time to Amanzimtoti, or 'Toti', only 12 miles south of Durban, of which it is effectively a suburb. The Zulu name translates as 'sweet waters', as described by Shaka.

We were invited to join our next-door neighbours, the Erasmuses, Ivor and Felicity plus their three children to play with Leon and Andrew, Julia was a little young to join in the fun. We stayed in separate beach-front apartments like thousands of local folk who spend their annual beach holiday there, swimming, soaking up the sun and partying.

Sporting facilities in Amanzimtoti were excellent and included tennis, golf, bowls and angling. Canoes and pedalos were also available for hire - something for everyone.

Ross Bartholomew, one of Leon's friends, remembers their childhood in Jagersfontein:

"My memories of Jagersfontein are many, though not very full. By this I mean that I can remember many things and events but certainly not in the sort of detail that would make for story reading.

My main friends were Leon, Peter Erasmus and Keith Canning. We interacted with others but these are the ones I got to know the best. We used to play a lot in the Square where we all lived. Riding bicycles or rollers skating or building soap-box carts that we diced down the Square hill and crashed into our garden at the bottom. Some of us kept silk-worms and these gave us some joy. One of them had drawers full of the worms and these fascinated us greatly. We would often play in the mine property behind the Square and had much fun there. Sometimes we would even go to the piggery and throw stones at the piglets to hear them screech.

I had a Boxer called Bruce and Leon had an Alsatian dog but I can't remember its name (by coincidence our dog was also Bruce). These two did not see eye to eye and were often in major fights which I can remember put much fear into us when trying to stop them.

I used to walk to and from school, but can't remember ever walking with anyone else. I used to stop at the butchery and was fascinated by all the meat being unloaded and especially the vast numbers of flies that used to gather in the blood tray hanging off the back of the truck. Then it was on to the local garage where I (almost on a daily basis) would ask if there were any new stickers. The STP one was my favourite at the time. Then on to school and just before I got there I would balance across a water pipe that crossed a gulley. On a recent visit to Jagers I saw the pipe and it obviously looked much shorter but no less formidable to cross. None of my children ventured to try!

At school there was much fun. We were four classes all together, Sub A & B as well as Std 1 & 2 (that would now be Grades 1 to 4) and our teacher was Mrs Opperman. At break time we used to swing like crazed people, trying to see if we could get the swing to go so high that they would go around the pole. Fortunately we never got this right as we would probably have severely hurt ourselves. We would also jump off the swings to see how far we could jump. I even participated in a school play and I was a monkey in a play called 'Willie Willie Wallie'.

On many Saturdays we would watch a movie at the City Hall. My parents would go to Charlesville to play tennis and I remember some of that.

Sometimes we would crawl along one of the gullies that would eventually come out into the mine hole (I don't think Leon was actually ever with me on these adventures). Once I was caught and had to face the music which actually heightened the excitement of the adventure.

Don't remember much more than that I am afraid."

With Ross talking about school I should refer to some of the school reports that I still have in my possession.

Leon's teacher at Jagers was Mrs Opperman, with a headmaster, Mr Ferreira. His subjects taken were religious instruction, Afrikaans, English, arithmetic, history and geography, woodwork, hygiene, writing, nature study and art. He averaged 70% in his subjects for two terms, which was good but inexplicably 55% in the middle term of three. That was mainly due to his arithmetic dropping from 67 out of 80 to only 29 out of 80. Difficult to believe but that is what the reports show.

My youngest son Andrew remembers Jagersfontein, "climbing on the roof, it was easy, as the garden must have been built up at the back, so it didn't seem so high. The drain-pipe at the back left-hand corner, gave easy access. I still have a scar to this day, from when I rushed to get down, maybe you or Mum were coming home and a piece of wire caught me on the ball bag and left a long cut ouch!!! (still a talking point on occasions). I remember Julia's cot being painted, white I think, in an outhouse, by the apricot tree. Yes,

I still love apricots from those days, climbing up and eating too many unripe ones. What was over the back of the house? I recall a dirt road, then a fence of some sort. Over the fence was a salt pan, dried up area, felt very off bounds to me as I explored.

There's a Beatles track " O bla di, oh bla da, life goes on, ohhh , la la la la life goes on, Jonny has a etc etc. I seem to attach this to a grocer's shop in the high street of Jagers and a pub with swing doors and the bank, the swimming pool and the country club. I do remember playing with some black kids on the outside of town, whipping a bike tire along; they seemed to laugh a lot."

I can also report a quite comical incident that occurred with Leon and Andrew at the doctor's surgery. Because there had been an epidemic of influenza at Jagers the previous year the mine had decided that all personnel, especially their children, should have a flu jab. I accompanied Leon and Andrew to see Dr Botha and as we walked into his surgery he asked who would like to be first to have the jab. Leon pushed Andrew forward to have the first shot. Unfortunately for Leon, just the sight of the needle entering his brother's arm made him faint. However, we couldn't let him get away with that reaction and he still had to take his medicine.

The truth was that Andrew never did show fear. He was as tough as they come. Although he was quite small, he had a big heart and would always give as good as he got, especially when he had to fight his way out of trouble. We still have a tape recording of him saying he wasn't scared of snakes and such-like and he was given the nickname of 'Tiger Thompson' which stayed with him for years.

In South Africa, it seemed that even Bruce and later, Taffy our dogs, knew the difference between black and white men. They knew that white men were in charge and that the black men were mainly servants. It had been that way for years.

One of the reasons that Bruce was against the blacks was a result of next door's butcher's boy attacking him with a stone. The stone was thrown at Bruce from outside our fence and cut his head open to the bone. After the attack by the butcher's boy we could see the sticky crimson blood oozing out of his skull. Something he would never forget. Every time the boy came anywhere near our property Bruce used to go wild, wanting to get at him to pay him back for the damage inflicted.

We made many friends at Jagersfontein.

Eddie and Pam Green. Eddie was the mine surveyor and both were always very helpful in times of crisis. Eddie also played a mean game of golf. Is that what they call a bandit?

Bill and Heather Bartholomew and son Ross. Bill was a mine shift-boss and a Springbok shottist, representing South Africa in several international shooting events. They lived at the bottom of the Mine Square.

Paul du Toit, mine manager, and his wife Dorothy. Both were bowlers and Dorothy also an angler. Their son, Douglas, learnt his swimming at Jagers.

In 1968 he was congratulated on his outstanding success in the Griqualand West championships for achieving four firsts, three seconds and one third despite having, on occasions, to swim in competition with adults. No wonder he was selected to swim in the Currie Cup series in Bloemfontein.

Dick and Maud Gore, the resident engineer and his wife, stalwarts of the Mine Square top hierarchy.

Dick Du Plessis ex mine captain who lived two doors above us. His son, Dickie, fancied my sister Sandra. His daughter Marie married Norman Chemaley who owned the town shop/café.

Ivor and Felicity Erasmus and their three kids David, Peter and Melany plus Felicity's mother Mrs Goodwin from Welkom Mine, secretary to Ron McKechnie (who I referred to in a previous chapter.)

Father Tim, the Roman Catholic priest, a friend of the Erasmuses and a very interesting character. He was one for the girls and obviously liked Iris, saying she was the spitting image of Julie Andrews. At Christmas Eve 1969 we were all invited to a party given by the Chemaleys, the owner of the café plus grocery in town. The event took place in their large garage where there was plenty of room for eating, drinking and dancing. Everyone enjoyed themselves, especially Father Tim, who showed he was a typical Irishman who enjoyed his drink, especially the black stuff, Guinness. As the time got closer to midnight one of his friends shouted to Tim that he must not forget he was due to conduct a Midnight Mass. I couldn't believe that Tim was fit to perform such a ceremony under the influence so I suggested to Iris that she should go along to see how he performed his duties. On her return from the Mass she was pleased to report that it was an excellent service and no sign that Tim had been drinking.

Conclusion - The last I heard was that he had left the Ministry and married a woman with six children. Well done Tim.

My underground foreman fitter, Willie Boshoff, whom I relied on heavily, still resides in Jagers and I was fortunate to meet up with him there during my visit in March 2008 to carry out the final research for my book.

Plant Supt Clive and Doreen Parker lived next door below us but I have been unable to trace them or their family.

Mine Captain Kobus van Jaarsveld and his wife Fienie and two children. He followed us to Finsch Mine but then his position in De Beers took off. He rose to general manager. Subsequently he became a consulting engineer for the diamond section of Anglo American Corporation.

Ernest Bailey. An excellent chap, a bowls colleague and former secretary of Jagers Mine who always had close contact with the top brass in Kimberley.

Karel Booysen, Archie Miller and Fanie Ackermann my underground fitter, electrician and rigger in that order. Of these three I was only able to track down Archie, who still works for De Beers in Kimberley at the old De Beers Country Club as a security manager. When I saw him during my visit he was easily recognisable by the large grin on his face and a drink in his hand.

Bill Le Barrow, his wife Betty and daughters Hope and Mary-Lynn.

(The following excerpts regarding Bill were found in the De Beers News from the Mines magazines)

"September 1967, W Le Barrow is a gifted writer and despite his handicap he is a highly skilled photographer. Men of his calibre are an asset to any community.

April 1968 Bill Le Barrow is stumbling about in his usual semi-comatose state after weeks of hospitalisation and recuperation.

July 1968 Bill Le Barrow has been discharged from hospital. He is recovering well and is keen to continue his history of Jagersfontein.

July 1971 It is with deep regret that we record the death of our Editor of Blougrond, Mr William Leonard Le Barrow on 12 May, 1971, in our local hospital (just two weeks before the mine closed down).

Bill started his Naval career with his basic training on the General Botha in 1929. During this period he was awarded the First Prize for Seamanship. On 10 April, 1931, he sustained severe back injuries, when his ship, the Cape St. Francis, was off loading at Colombo Harbour (Ceylon). As a result of this accident, Bill was unable to continue service at sea and joined the New Jagersfontein Mining and Exploration Co. He was transferred to Koffiefontein Mine during 1937 and remained there until closing down in 1940. At this time, Bill recuperated sufficiently to be able to return to sea, serving in the Merchant Navy as a second officer, until he was discharged as medically unfit in 1946.

The town witnessed what is claimed to be Africa's first air fatality in 1892, 12 years before the Wright brothers took to the air. Mr Bill le Barrow, the town's unofficial historian and most loyal son, retold the story shortly before his death in Jagersfontein hospital last month. An intrepid balloonist, Harry Goodall, watched by his wife and a crowd of miners, took off from a kloof just north of the town; a crosswind whipped his balloon over a hill, dragging his body across the rock-strewn, volcanic hillside until it was caught in a bush."

An unenviable task I was forced to perform at the mine was the sacking of a winding engine driver. I received a call late at night from the security office at the entrance gate to the mine, who reported that a temporary driver working on the Man Hoist, of all places, was suspected of being under the influence of drink. When I arrived at the gate I was surprised that they had let him in. I found the man at work on the hoist. In speaking to him and smelling his breath it was obvious the guard was correct. I told him to stop operating the machine and escorted him back to security where I told him that his services were no longer required and he would be receiving official notification in the morning. I then managed to obtain another person able to operate the hoist until the end of the night shift.

One of the worst nights of my life occurred at Jagers when Dick Gore was on leave and I was acting R.E. The problem was due to the steam boilers overheating, resulting in the dramatic noise of the power station alarm sirens, similar to the ones emitted during World War Two. When the alarm went off I was actually in the bath relaxing after a hard day's graft. The lights went out and within seconds the sirens started. Iris managed to find some candles and I was able to dress quickly and jump into my Austin car to drive to the power station. Fortunately, my foreman Willy Boshoff was already there and had taken control. It took probably 15 minutes to ascertain the cause of the problem. The boiler attendant had been unable to see the water level in the boiler sight glasses and had assumed, wrongly, that water wasn't getting to the boilers as normal. By incorrectly turning off the wrong valves he had succeeded in starving the system, hence the alarms going off.

One of my saddest memories relates to the fact that nothing can be more stupid and obstinate than a flock of sheep. I was driving from Bloemfontein to Jagersfontein late one evening and came across a large number of sheep. I slowed down hoping they would make room for the car but one just decided to jump in front of the car at the last minute. The unfortunate animal was injured but what could we do? After Iris's experience with the springbok and blesbok she couldn't stand the thought of anyone slaughtering it and us preparing a meal from such a defenceless creature. We also had no idea where the farmer who owned the livestock lived or how to contact him. The only thing we could think of at the time was to drag it into the ditch that ran alongside the dirt road hoping that the farmer would be able to find it before someone or something else removed it for the pot. After that, it was a case of peering into the darkness ahead, searching the road for obstacles, especially more sheep. It wasn't much of a road - a track ploughed out of the red earth and eroded into corrugations by the rain and traffic.

In 1968 Jagers was one the most civilized centres in Orange Free State, outside of Bloemfontein. A fortress of its own well out into the country, with its private gardens, tennis courts, lawn bowling green and golf course. It was here that the South African and European community met on long winter evenings to read plays. Examples were:

Dec 1961 "For Pete's Sake" by Leslie Sands - A Family Frolic - A full three act play produced by Henry Stucke

May 1963 "Wanted One Body" by Raymond Dyer produced by Henry Stucke

May 1964 "Mad About Men" by Peter Blackmore produced by Henry Stucke

May 1965 "My Fair Lady" by George Bernard Shaw produced by Bill Le Barrow

Dec 1965 "Flat Spin" by Derek Royle - A Farcical Comedy produced by Hubert Wright

Apr 1968 "Miss Pel is Missing" - Also there were readings in both languages.

I was asked to appear in the play reading for May 1969, playing opposite our next door neighbour Felicity. All we players had were our own personalities, with what understandings and theatrical memories we had acquired through the years. It was reassuring to discover what a vivid social life was possible under those circumstances. On the night of our reading we were handed sheets of paper containing our parts and directed to read those parts. We grew into our parts as the night progressed. As we ended our reading there was genuine applause, especially when I had to kiss Felicity on stage. Our audience was grateful that, for a few hours, we had provided them with an escape from their humdrum everyday life.

We also joined most of the town to watch bioscope (films) every Saturday night. One incident to remember was when Hilmary Hodgson, wife of Norman of the engineering staff, returned home only to find that the keys she needed were in her handbag which she had left at the Town Hall. She woke up the caretaker who unlocked the hall to find the handbag still at her seat. I am sure the chances of that happening today are not so good. Other happenings which will be of interest were Otto Roux, the extremely large hoist driver, who would shout out warnings to the cowboy in the picture that some crooks were going to shoot him. He was really carried away with the excitement. Also if one sat next to Millie Andrews, the wife of Alf Andrews, Engineering Foreman, one would hear a running commentary of the picture, whether one liked it or not.

There are freak diamonds so large or unusual that they become legend. Diamonds that have their own names, with histories that are recorded and invested with romance. The great 'paragons' - stones of the first water, whose cut and finished weight exceed 100 carats. Jagersfontein has produced many of them. The Jubilee diamond, a superb 245-carat cushion of unearthly fire fashioned out of a 650-carat rough - then the biggest of them all at the mine the

Excelsior. This stone at 995.2 carats was the largest that had yet been discovered. Only the famous Cullinan diamond of 3,106 carats, retrieved from Premier Mine in 1905 was to surpass it. Besides, it was not only a diamond of exceptional quality but it was a rare 'blue white' - a colour for which Jagersfontein was justly famous.

Before finishing this part of the story in Jagersfontein, I want to touch on my realisation of the family image created by De Beers throughout the mines under their control - from boys and girls leaving school where the top pupils gained their De Beers Diamond scholarships or began apprenticeships with excellent training at both external training centres and at De Beers own training schools. Top scholars, showing management material, were sent to first-class universities and colleges both in South Africa, normally Wits University, and possibly the UK - Cambridge, or the USA - Harvard. No expense was spared to ensure the lines of authority and control were maintained at present and well into the future. On reaching employment on the mines all employees were encouraged to join sports and leisure clubs unrivalled anywhere else in the world e.g. at Jagers yacht, theatre, Diggers cricket and rugby clubs, badminton, tennis, bowls, swimming, golf, angling and pistol shooting.

At Kimberley we had De Beers soccer and hockey clubs, cycling, squash, cricket, swimming club, several bowls clubs, not to mention scouts, cubs, girl guides, pony club etc. Those fortunate enough to be a manager or engineer would probably have a welcoming celebration to meet all colleagues prior to starting work; a presentation party on leaving to go to another property of De Beers or AAC; three to six weeks' annual holidays plus long leave after five years. This was topped up by excellent living quarters, choice of motor car etc, 10 year-long continuous service ties and, after 25 years service, an inscribed gold watch from the Chairman, Harry Oppenheimer. Top management also had many extra-mural jobs such as chairman or member of committees which ensured that all would follow in the De Beers template which endeared them to the community.

Blacks and Coloureds also had their rewards for being employees of De Beers, with their training, free meals during their contracts, bonuses for handing in diamonds picked up off the floor in the mine, length of service awards, membership of first aid, ambulance teams and sports clubs run by the hostel management. Even when they retired they were always invited to a Christmas party to celebrate their time with De Beers.

This is partly demonstrated in an address, given by Paul du Toit on the transfer of the mine manager Hugh Allen from Jagers to Anglo American Corporation. He remarked that both mine and town were losing a man who had capably accomplished a lot for both, and observed that the all-round experience gained in Jagers had served many who were now highly placed officials in Anglo-American, such as Messrs Gallagher Hartley, Hunt, Gyngell, West and Stucke. However, Mr. Allen was going to a good mine with a reliable staff, and he wished him all success and congratulated him on his new venture. Concluding, Mr. du Toit expressed his pleasure and satisfaction on returning to Jagers and after welcoming pensioners to the party, presented Mr. Allen with a splendid briefcase.

Resident engineer Dick Gore, cricket club chairman, also made a presentation on behalf of the cricketers.

In reply, Mr. Allen expressed thanks for the party and gifts. During their 18 months' stay he and Mrs. Allen had made warm and close friendships among the small community of a nature impossible to achieve in a city. They would miss this greatly. The friendly co-operation of all, the large herds of blesbok, which are a distinction of this property, and the birth of their son here would keep Jagers indelibly impressed in their memories.

Concluding, Mr. Allen said that Jagers mine would celebrate its centenary in 1971, a very old mine for this country, which had produced the finest diamonds in the world. He was indeed proud to have served on this famous mine.

After just 13 months at Jagers I was again transferred: this time to Finsch Mine, 200 miles away north west of Kimberley with a promotion to Earthmoving Section Engineer of what was then the largest opencast diamond mine in the world. I was leaving the largest hand-dug diamond mine and I still have very fond memories of Jagers, but within 18 months the mine would be closed.

CLOSING DOWN OF JAGERSFONTEIN MINE (extracts from De Beers' archives)

"It was Friday afternoon, the 28 May, 1971, approaching 4.30 pm. The afternoon was a slightly chilly one as the visiting dignitaries and officials made their way to their seats after visiting the engine room to see the rock winder carry out its last remaining tasks.

On either side of the dais seating accommodation was arranged for the visitors and mine personnel and their families. Many mine Europeans and Africans stood in a wide semi-circle to observe the last official function of the Jagersfontein Mine.

This was the setting when the Manager, Mr Miller welcomed the Resident Director, Mr A. S. Hall, Mr and Mrs Borchers. Dr Raath, Mr R. Daniel and Mr C. West.

In his address. Mr Miller referred to the mine being a little over 100 years old. It was discovered in 1870 and proclaimed in 1871 when hundreds of men emerged on the area, staking their claims and working in the open pit. Small companies were formed until 1877 when the New Jagersfontein Mining and Exploration Company was formed and it was in 1891 when they gained complete control of the Mine.

In 1893, the biggest find of the mine was made - the Excelsior, a blue white diamond weighing 972 carats.

Opencast work carried on until the Boer War during which time it was flooded. Operations again commenced after the war; in 1904 the main shaft was commenced and commissioned in 1911 and

118

the steam hoist which was installed is still in operation today. The mine continued to function until 1914 and was again closed during the war years. The labour force at the mine was 781 Europeans and 7000 Africans.

The chambering method of mining was employed until the mid fifties when a change was made to block cave methods.

During the period 1887 to 1932. the mine produced 7.5 million carats. When the mine was reopened in 1949, it produced until 1971 a further 2.25 million carats. Based on 1970 values, the total value of the proclamation was R260,000,000 (£130M at 1968 rates).

TRIBUTES

Mr Miller paid a warm tribute to the pioneers of the early days and then to all those personnel with whom he was closely associated over the past one and three quarter years. He thanked the Consulting Engineers for their assistance, also the General Manager, Mr D. Borchers and the Assistant General Manager, Mr D. Rankin. He also paid tribute to his staff; Mr D. Gore, the Resident Engineer and his Foremen and Artisans; Mine Captain Kruger and all those personnel who worked with him. He thanked the Plant Personnel for their efficient operations and high recovery as well as the backroom boys in the stores and secretarial administration.

In concluding his address, he wished all those personnel who were leaving, luck in their future ventures and extended a similar wish as well as one of prosperity, to the residents of Jagersfontein

Mr D. Borchers, General Manager of De Beers Consolidated Mines. Limited, thanked on behalf of the Company to which he referred as a great company, everyone for the work done for Jagersfontein Mine and the Group as a whole.

Mr Borchers, a man of many years experience in the mining industry, and as one who has often witnessed the closing of mines, was therefore qualified to express the thoughts of mining men and the close relationship that existed between them and the mine. Because of this relationship and the manner in which men identified themselves with a mine, he said it was upsetting for any man not to remain unemotional about the closing down of a mine, particularly such a wonderful mine as Jagersfontein. He paid warm tribute to the fantastic efforts made by those who were dead and gone, those who had retired, and those who had worked right up until the last shift.

In concluding his address, Mr Borchers expressed his thoughts in a manner which was a tribute to both the mining industry and the men who unstintingly served this great industry.

THE LAST SKIP

At the conclusion of his address, Mr Miller called upon the banksman, Mr P. van Loggerenburg, to signal to the driver, Mr Otto Roux, for the last skip. It was a poignant moment when the last skip slowly ascended, the steam hoist fulfilling its last function after serving decades of mechanical perfection, and the final load was tipped for treatment in the plant. To the hissing of steam issuing from the hoist and the shrill blast of the hooter, there was the accompanying applause of the audience."

Chapter Six

Finsch Mine, Lime Acres, N Cape: October 1969 to November 1970

THE HISTORY OF FINSCH MINE (Extracts from Finsch Mine archives)

In the late 1930s a farm called Brits, some 37 miles east of Postmasburg, was reputed to contain yellow ground indicating the presence of kimberlite. This was confirmed in prospecting pits by Danie de Bruyn in 1957 but not further explored because all precious stones rights belonged to the State, In 1958, a Mr Schwabel, employed by a prospector Mr Fincham, prospecting for crocidolite asbestos, recognised garnet kimberlite indicator minerals in De Bruyn's pits.

The Precious Stones Act was amended in 1960 and after the base-metal rights had lapsed. Finsch Diamonds was formed in May 1961 to prospect for diamonds, the name being derived from the first three letters of surnames of Fincham and Schwabel. In November 1961 a 0.75 carat stone was found in the first wash. The mine was proclaimed in 1962 and Fincham's Discoverer's Certificate was ceded to Finsch Diamonds in 1963. In May 1964 all the shares and rights of Finsch Diamonds were bought by De Beers Consolidated Mines Limited for R4.5million and overburden stripping started.

The kimberlite treatment plant became operational in 1966. Full production was achieved in 1967 from truck and shovel open pit bench mining methods. The open pit ceased operations in September 1990. All of the tonnage is now mined from underground by an open stope mining system.

Nearly 110 million tons of waste rock and nearly 98 million tons of diamond bearing kimberlite were mined from the open pit to produce almost 79 million carats.

In 1995 the mine was the largest underground producer of diamonds at 1,722,597 carats from 3,496,000 tons treated."

In 1969 I was appointed as the section engineer responsible primarily for the maintenance of the massive earth-moving fleet dedicated to the removal of millions of tons of diamond-bearing ore and waste rock. My foremen were Dick Wilson, in charge of the maintenance of the earth-moving equipment, and Sonny Stein, overseeing the general support vehicles and cars, vans and fleet of Land Rovers. To give you some idea of the size of the task, my annual budget was more than £1,000,000 (R2,000,000) including capital costs for the fleet.

The mine manager was Gerald Claughton BSc Mining (Leeds) from Lancashire and the resident engineer was Jim Burgess from Scotland. The plant superintendent was Andrew Parker from Kimberley.

Finsch mine was the biggest opencast diamond mine in the world at that time. I was responsible for the buying and maintenance of excavators, dump trucks, road scrapers front end loaders, scrapers, etc and the involvement in setting up and developing fleet maintenance procedures. Putting the procedures into practice proved problematical in that planned changes of equipment based on fixed hours or mileage resulted in good equipment being replaced by inferior equipment. This was primarily due to poor re-engineering at the suppliers that eventually resulted in excessive downtime, which started to affect production at the mine.

Special Investigations -

1) Survey into the number and size of dumptrucks required until the end of the life of the mine.

2) Implementation of Planned Preventative Maintenance

The Thompsons Journey
Through South Africa

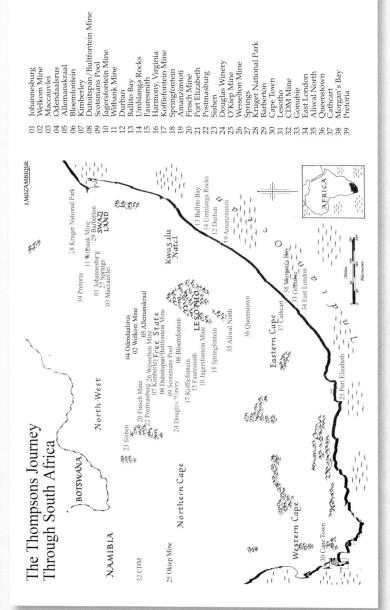

01 Johannesburg
02 Welkom Mine
03 Maccauvlei
04 Odendaalsrus
05 Allemanskraal
06 Bloemfontein
07 Kimberley
08 Dutoitspan/Bultfontein Mine
09 Scotsmans Pool
10 Jagersfontein Mine
11 Witbank Mine
12 Durban
13 Ballito Bay
14 Umhlanga Rocks
15 Fauresmith
16 Harmony, Virginia
17 Koffiefontein Mine
18 Springfontein
19 Amanzimtoti
20 Finsch Mine
21 Port Elizabeth
22 Postmasburg
23 Sishen
24 Douglas Winery
25 O'Kiep Mine
26 Wesselton Mine
27 Springs
28 Kruger National Park
29 Barberton
30 Cape Town
31 Lesotho
32 CDM Mine
33 Gonubie
34 East London
35 Aliwal North
36 Queenstown
37 Cathcart
38 Morgan's Bay
39 Pretoria

Map showing mines worked at and places visited 1966 to 1973.

Cecil Rhodes and co-founders of De Beers
at Board meeting 1893 in Kimberley. *Page 86*

Kimberley Mine roadway 1890s. *Page 67*

Cecil Rhodes. *Page 69*

Ernest Oppenheimer. *Page 72*

Harry Oppenheimer. *Page 75*

Nicky Oppenheimer. *Page 75*

Kimberley Market Square 1880s. *Page 65*

Two diamond sorters at work 1890s. *Page 68*

A view of
Kimberley Mine
1873. *Page 79*

First Diamond
Washing Machine
1870s. *Page 68*

Early Diamond
Washing Gear
1870s. *Page 68*

Kimberley
Mine early days
1870s. *Page 79*

Leon, Julia and Andrew by Bill le Barrow 1969. *Page 106*

Andrew with boxing gloves 1969.
Page 109

Yours truly De Beers 1970.

Andrew, Mum, Leon, Ross and Peter at Jagersfontein 1969. *Page 101*

Rodger Symcox, father of Patrick and my best bowls friend. *Page 177*

Aerial view of the Open Mine at Jagersfontein 1966. *Page 95*

Aerial view of Mine Square Jagersfontein 1966
(arrow showing No 8 Mine Square). *Page 92*

Jack Woodburne, Jim and Moira Burgess, Len and Iris Thompson
at DBCC 1971. *Page 141*

LT, Elbie de Klerk, Lyall Bennetto and Terry Freeme
at Cape Town 1971. *Page 147*

Daphne Richards, Iris and Judy Ellett at Kimberley
Art Museum 1970. *Page 80*

Lesotho diamond 1970s. *Page 157*

LT De Beers Country Club Mens'
Singles Bowls Champion 1971. *Page 142*

LT with air rifle 1968. *Page 41*

Julia 5-years old in Chesterfield.

World famous 'Big Hole' in Kimberley. *Page 69*

Flamingos on water pan 1966. *Page 32*

Thompson family at 16 Zomba Street Welkom 1967. *Page 36*

Volcanic disturbances that placed kimberlite in the earth's crust. *Page 79*

Leon, Andrew and Bruce
the Alsatian 1969. *Page 109*

Sandra and Leon ready for Rickshaw
ride with Zulu in Durban 1969. *Page 100*

Grandad Stone, Leon, Andrew and Julia. *Page 160*

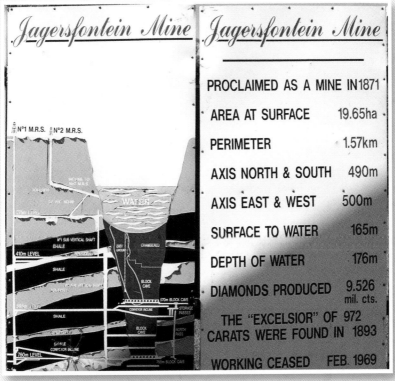

Jagersfontein Mine

N°1 M.R.S.　N°2 M.R.S.

WATER

N°1 SUB VERTICAL SHAFT
SHALE
410m LEVEL
SHALE
SHALE
760m LEVEL

GRAVEL GROUND
CHAMBERED
BLOCK CAVE
570m BLOCK CAVE
CONVEYOR INCLINE
STORAGE PASSES
BLOCK CAVE
NORTH PASS
760m BLOCK CAVE

Jagersfontein Mine

PROCLAIMED AS A MINE IN 1871

AREA AT SURFACE   19.65ha

PERIMETER   1.57km

AXIS NORTH & SOUTH   490m

AXIS EAST & WEST   500m

SURFACE TO WATER   165m

DEPTH OF WATER   176m

DIAMONDS PRODUCED   9.526
                     mil. cts.

THE "EXCELSIOR" OF 972
CARATS WERE FOUND IN 1893

WORKING CEASED   FEB. 1969

Cross-section of Jagersfontein mine 1969. *Page 86*

A typical blast at Finsch Mine to remove the diamond ore
for treatment and recovery of the diamonds. *Page 132*

A 'soldier' termite (left), stands on a minute yellow diamond that 'worker' termites have brought up from the depths below. Termites such as these provide De Beers geologists with some of their first clues that diamond pipes were there. *Page 138*

The aerial view of Finsch Mine showing the excavations after 30 years of working of the open pit. *Page 121*

Diamond cutting process
of the Earth Star diamond,
images 1 to 6. *Page 102*

Image 1.

Image 2.

Image 3.

Image 4.

Image 5.

Image 6.

Sorting diamonds. *Page 188*

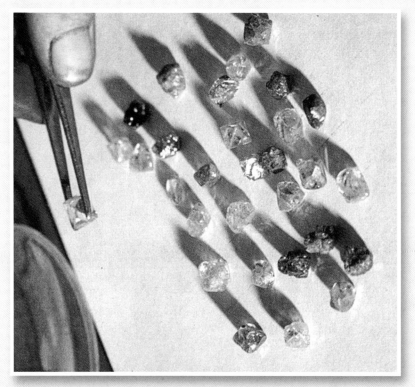

Assortment of diamonds at De Beers Kimberley. *Page 188*

Diamond collection. *Page 188*

Five beautiful diamonds on a hand from De Beers. *Page 188*

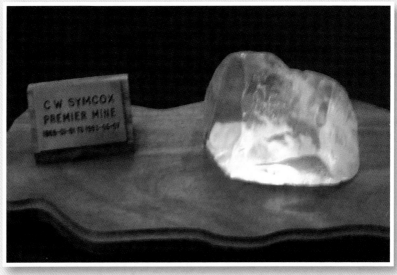

Cullinan replica 3106-carat diamond presented to my friend Weston Symcox at Premier Mine. *Page 116*

The 650.80-carat Jubilee diamond was discovered at Jagersfontein Mine 1895 and presented to Queen Victoria to celebrate her Diamond Jubilee. *Page 115*

A stone embedded in 'blueground' rock. *Page 188*

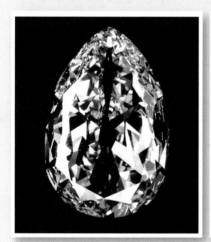

The 972-carat Excelsior diamond found in 1893 at Jagersfontein mine, which is renowned for having produced many large stones. *Page 116*

The De Beers diamond, initially 428.5-carats holds the title of being the fourth largest cut diamond in the world at 228.5-carats.

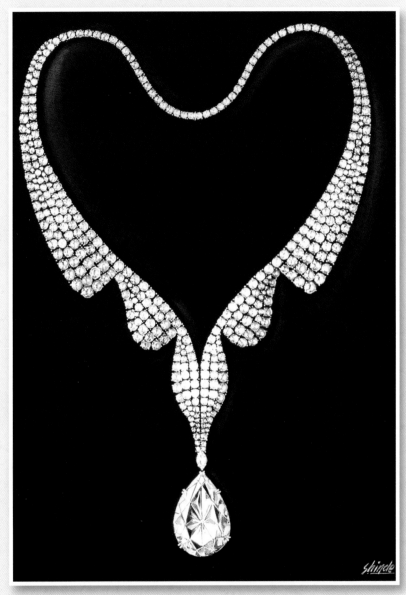

Elizabeth Taylor wore the Taylor-Burton Diamond, given
to her by Richard Burton, in a necklace by Cartier.

Scheme based mainly on the replacement of vehicle sub-assemblies according to their anticipated degree of wear thus pre-empting catastrophic breakdown with consequent expensive repair/replacement together with disruption of haulage operations.

During April 1970 it was decided that with all the high-powered diesel equipment under my control it made sense for me to attend a two week Detroit Diesel Training course at Port Elizabeth for diesel engine monitoring and control. This certainly helped my understanding of my foremen and mechanics day to day problems in greater detail and helped to formulate improvements in our testing procedures of the diesel engines in operation at Finsch.

Although I worked at Finsch mine for more than a year I never saw a diamond in its natural environment but saw plenty of diamonds, after the recovery process. Particularly one day, we were having a meeting in the board room and the plant superintendent Andrew Parker brought in a bowl full of diamonds, part of the day's production, and poured them out onto the open table. They were just like granules of sugar since 90 per cent of the diamonds found at Finsch mine were industrial i.e. too small for the jewellery market. Andrew advised me that the diamonds recovered from the top levels were occasionally green in colour.

Lime Acres was a town comprised of personnel working for two organisations. The first was Northern Lime, a company producing lime and other products from their quarry within three miles of the Finsch mine, employing probably half the number of employees working at the De Beers property.

On arrival at Lime Acres from Jagers they didn't have a house available in our required category so we had to stay in a foreman-type accommodation until they had built us a brand new engineer's house, which was to take six months.

The first house was just a standard three bedroom brick-built bungalow with smallish kitchen, dining room and lounge. The front and back gardens were very run-down, mostly lawn with a few bushes here and there. A drive ran the whole length of the property to a double garage, required for our Ford 17M and a Land Rover allocated to me by the mine.

One of the problems we were faced with in our stay there was the poor access to fresh milk. For some reason the mine doctor, Doctor Mills, had sent a sample of milk off for testing at a laboratory. When the results came back there were traces of TB, bacillus and other nasty bugs so the doctor advised everyone to boil their milk. But in our case we were told not to give it to Julia and he only recommended powdered milk. Apparently even boiling it did not guarantee getting rid of all the bugs. Therefore while we lived in Lime Acres poor Julia had to make do with powdered milk until we returned to Kimberley.

Our dog Bruce was an excellent guard dog and we all doted on him. However his character changed after we moved to Lime Acres when one day a Bantu maid was just walking past our property and for some reason Bruce took an immediate dislike to her, probably as a result of the attack on him by the butcher's boy at Jagers. As she passed our front gate, Bruce jumped over our 4ft high wire fence with ease, chased after her and bit the woman on the leg. I had to take her to our doctor for a tetanus jab and apologised profusely for Bruce's actions.

Unfortunately that was a step, or a jump, too far for Bruce and next day I took him in my car and deposited him at the nearest SPCA asking them if they could find a good farm nearby for a superior guard dog, where I hoped he would be well looked after. Strangely it took Leon and Andrew two days before they realised that Bruce had gone and missed him bitterly until I got a replacement when we were later transferred back to Kimberley.

Early in our stay at Lime Acres Iris was thrilled, as we all were, when passing her driving test nearly forty miles away at Postmasburg, the nearest testing station. The place could be described in those days as a one horse town, a single square of houses, no traffic lights, no hills to do a hill-start, no pavements in which to do a three-point turn. Just a drive round the square, answer a few Highway Code questions and pass paper signed and delivered. Since I couldn't get away from work at the time Iris went with a friend of ours Natalie Dabner, the wife of the Finsch boilermaker foreman Johnny.

However, Iris upset me by saying that she had learnt more from Natalie in those two hours of the journey than the whole 18 months I had been teaching her how to drive at Jagersfontein.

So I will be happy to put the following down to Natalie's influence:

After we had moved to the new house, Iris reversed along the long drive to go to town but crashed into the gatepost and could not go forward or reverse without causing more damage. However, she was fortunate to have a group of African workers passing by at the time and they were kind enough to lift the Ford 17M car, very heavy, away from the gate to enable Iris to drive back towards our garage.

Iris warned the children not to tell me about the accident until after I had my evening meal, for fear of affecting my digestion. However, Andrew, the little monkey, just couldn't wait to tell me at the dining table. He brought out a sizable piece of red plastic out of his pocket saying, 'Look what mum's done to your car', followed by squeals of laughter from both children. As usual my main concern was for their welfare and I said as long as no one was hurt it didn't matter.

Iris always said that I was not blameless, having scraped the car on the evening of our leaving Kruger Park. I explain this away through having driven over 200 miles in my rushed attempt to get out of the Park before the deadline and trying to get home before it was dark. We had to stop overnight half-way at a motel and as it was getting dusk I narrowly scraped the front off-side of the Ford on a vertical post supporting one of their car ports but no real damage.

Mine captain Kobus van Jaarsveld and his wife Fienie and two children followed us to Lime Acres from Jagers and we renewed our friendship with each other. However this didn't last long. We invited Kobus and Fienie one night to the old house, just across the road from their brand new one, for dinner. Iris went to a lot of trouble to impress them with her cooking, serving several dishes. At the end of the meal we retired into the lounge for liqueurs and Iris had included in her shopping the Dutch liqueur Van der Hum, liked by the majority of our few Afrikaans friends. Unfortunately, looking back at the event, we must have had one or two drinks too many because we started talking about the Boer War. It turned out that, I think it was one or two of Fienie's grandparents who were actually captured and put into a concentration camp where they died. From that night on the Van Jaarsvelds never gave us the time of day and we are still unsure of what was said to turn our friends into silent enemies.

Shortly after we moved into our newly-built house, just the other side of the van Jaarsvelds' house, our sixth move if we include the hotel in Welkom after a six months' wait. It was an obvious improvement on the first house at Lime Acres. First of all it was a double storey, unusual in South Africa, with four bedrooms, bathroom and separate shower, large kitchen and separate lounge and dining room with a spacious hall. The majority of the downstairs flooring was wooden blocks that necessitated the purchase of a floor polisher. There was a large stoep leading off the lounge which led to an extensive garden. The gardens were obviously new and we prepared the design, bought the required trees and bushes to set the gardening wheels in motion, all the hard work being done by a garden boy, initially employed seven days per week. Directly across the road outside our house was the open veld where Leon and Andrew loved to explore its sparse vegetation existing in the semi-arid conditions by its proximity to the Kalahari.

To celebrate our move into the new house we had to have a

house-warming party and we had plenty of help in its organisation from our new-found friends, mainly from the engineering side of the mine.

This was where I was introduced to the serious side of braaivleis (barbecue) using natural resources from the veldt, special tree or bush roots advised by John Dabner the foreman boilermaker and roasting on a spit supplied by the foreman carpenter Pete van Eyck. John took me deep into the veld in search of the special roots of a bush which once you had it burning would stay alight all night. Ideal for providing braaivleis meat for a large gathering.

There was no difficulty in providing as much drink as the occasion required since the suppliers to the mine were only too keen in competing to offer the liquid refreshments to make a party go with a bang. This would consist of Castle and Lion lagers, whisky, gin and Cinzano and brandy for the ladies. Pete also provided a speaker system so we could dance the night away with favourite tunes at the time such as Pretty Belinda etc. Needless to say, a good night was had by all.

Having learnt my early bowls at Jagersfontein I soon joined the Lime Acres Bowls Club which had both De Beers and Northern Lime employees making up the club with plenty of experienced bowlers to benefit from. Now I started playing bowls in earnest most Saturdays and Sundays and during the week in club competitions. Bowls at Jagers had involved playing against local clubs. The main difference at Lime Acres was we had to travel greater distances, up to 100 miles to play a game against clubs such as Sishen, Kimberley etc. However, one of the highlights of playing away was a visit to Douglas to play in their Open day for their Colemburg Trophy. We fielded very good sides probably due to the sponsors being a wine making company who supplied up to 60 bottles of wine as prizes for their various competitions. Since our bowlers won most of the competitions it resulted in the majority of the bottles of wine being drunk on the trip back home on the bus and needless to say everyone

127

enjoyed themselves.

This was confirmed in the News of the Mines magazine of November 1970, 'Congratulations to Elbie de Kock, Len Thompson, Edwina Every, and Miriam Deetlefs on winning the Culemborg Sponsored Day Trophy at Douglas. We sent five teams and had a most enjoyable time.'

The December issue had another bowls entry, 'Congratulations to the following on being selected to represent our Club in the Nationals at Cape Town next year, Lyall Bennetto, Elbie de Kock, Andre de Reuck, Terry Freeme and Len Thompson.' This actually took place in 1971 when we had moved back to Kimberley so I will pick up the story in the next chapter.

The following is the contribution of memories from my younger son Andrew:

Hi Dad, mmm, where to begin. Well how about the water tower, on the koppie across from our second house in Finsch. As a four year old, this seemed huge and quite a walk from the house, how far was it? My childhood perception is that it would have taken 10 minutes walking, so for my daughter Madeline that's about 600 metre ish. Anyway the water tower definitely seemed a dangerous and exciting place to visit. On one occasion as we were heading up the hill, we heard a truck and all (not sure who was there besides Leon and I, may be two or three other kids) so we hid behind bushes as the truck went past, full of African workers, laughing and joking. As a four year old boy, I looked up at these men, from my hidey hole and truly believed that if they caught us, we would be kidnapped and taken far away. So successfully avoiding their capture sticks with me to this day. As for the tower, well we used to try and climb up the ladder, but as I recall there was some barbed wire as you got to main cylinder, preventing us going any further.

My mind set at the time, was definitely that of 'the great white explorer, boldly going into the veld, with knife, stick, or any other weapon one could carry.' On one occasion, we went much further than ever before and came across a large hole in the dirt, which had a yellow bulldozer stuck in it. As well as the potential to get stuck in one of the many holes scattered around the bush, we also engaged the odd scorpion (I think).

Were we friendly with a doctor who lived up the street from us in Finsch? I can vividly remember, looking through a cupboard in his house with his son and finding these medical syringes. Great fun, the biggest made exceptional water pistols. Of course it wasn't stealing because we were just playing with them. Our other neighbours, the one with the maroon vintage car (South Africans), they had an enormous bag of monkey nuts, which came in handy for nourishment on our trips out into the bush. We used to hang out with Warren Symcox, back then; he was only five or six. I can vividly recall your Land Rover, with its the yellow and red gear knobs and trips up to the open cast mine to see half the hillside be blown apart, and the golf course which seemed to have a lot of snake holes. Mmmmm, seems like a long time ago now.

Most of this may not be relevant for the book, but it's good to put it down and for you to make some sense of my jumbled recollections. Love Andy

Son Leon's memories of Finsch:

"I remember in Finsch we used to go roaming round the streets looking for stuff to do. On one occasion about eight of us came across a scorpion, big black one. We would get in a circle around the scorpion and take it in turns to see who could get nearest or who could jump over it and the lower you jumped the more points you scored. This looking back, was very scary, as most of us went around with no shoes on and that scorpion knowing it was surrounded had its tail up and was aiming to get one of us if it could.

Andrew and I used to play Batman and Robin and we used to take it quite seriously. We figured that to save the world we would have to go out at night and deal with the baddies. Well this is exactly what we did on one occasion that I remember. Somehow one of us woke up at 2am or thereabouts and woke the other one up. We climbed out of the bedroom window and went to knock on the window of the other person (another kid) who we were playing the game with. We wondered the streets and there wasn't a soul in sight. Really quiet with big stars above. So still. We came across a night watchman that used to patrol the streets. He was mad at us for being out at that time of night and kept on telling us to go back, which we eventually did. I can't remember if he had a uniform on or not, but he had a truncheon. It's amazing to think of roaming streets so empty at that time. Nowadays it would be extremely dangerous in most parts of the world and there are generally people about as one goes home, but there wasn't anyone about in those days except for that night watchman.

We used to go on big expeditions in the bush which started outside our house and we would make for the water tower to start with. We used to love to climb it and look out over the scrub. We were aware that we had to keep an eye out for jeeps coming from the mine as they would have spotted us and would be coming to tell us off. We used to be able to track them by the dust that they made as they sped along. We would then climb down and head out further into the scrub. One good game we used to play was to get hold of one of the bush cows that roamed out there. These cows weren't anything the size of cows in England, much smaller probably because there wasn't much to eat out there. Probably about 4 foot high. We used to hold the cow by its neck and sides while someone helped another onto the cow. Everyone would then move away from the cow, and the cow would realise that it was free, but it also had someone on its back holding onto its neck for dear life. The cow would turn one way then the other but couldn't shake the person off. Eventually it would start running and they would generally head straight for a big thorn bush. The cows seemed to know this would get people off; maybe they evolved this idea from us or from whatever I don't know. The idea for us was simple. See how long you can stay on before the cow hits the bush. Great game full off laughter, fear and adrenaline. "

The swimming pool at Lime Acres was only small but ideal for teaching youngsters and that is where I taught Andrew. The lessons were very simple. First thing was to teach him to float through the water by me propelling him with his head down about 4 yards or so to the corner stairs of the pool. This gave him the confidence, not that he required it after his escapades at Umhlanga Rocks, of feeling safe in the pool. This was followed by him doing the same action but this time with his head above water. The next step was to push him with less force and tell him to stroke the last yard to the stairs. This method was repeated until he could manage the four yards without any assistance from me. He was then able to join Leon who taught him a lot more before we obtained professional coaching for them both on our return to Kimberley.

Stories I picked up about events in Lime Acres during my research done in March 2008.

The Chairman, Mr H. F. Oppenheimer opened the Coloured Primary School and also the Lime Acres Golf Club on Saturday, 16 November, 1968 and the same afternoon drove the first ball in a Nine Hole Golf Competition.

Mr Oppenheimer announced the opening of the clubhouse and then setup his ball on the first tee a distance of 240 metres to the first hole.

All the golf caddies stood at about the 200 metre mark, near the first bunker, waiting for the first ball to arrive.

The chairman, obviously nervous, swung at the ball and nearly hit a fresh air, the ball coming off the tee and bobbling along just a few yards from the tee. Andrew Parker was the only person who realised the chairman's predicament and politely applauded his effort.

However the ball was retrieved and the chairman was allowed to tee-off with a second chance. This time he hit the ball better but hooked it into the long grass and it took the numerous caddies some time to find his ball, with the finder duly rewarded.

After completion of the first hole, the chairman duly retired to the bar for congratulatory refreshments and this same ball was later installed in a glass presentation case at the entrance to the Finsch Mine office.

It wasn't there long before my Earthmoving foreman fitter, a naughty boy, took it into his head to replace the ball by borrowing the key to the case and replacing the golf ball by a set of old false teeth. What a cheek or a set of hollow cheeks (without the teeth).

Story of the Finsch Mine blasting joke on the chief storekeeper.

This is the story about Aubrey Duncan the one-armed, lovable but cantankerous at times manager of the main stores at Finsch mine.

Aubrey had few friends and many so-called enemies who loved to play jokes on him to repay him for his belligerence when dealing with customers at his stores.

Finsch mine used to blast rock two or three times a week and each blast could remove many thousand tons from the in-situ rock.

The mine employed a two-minute warning siren, operated prior to blasting, to enable employees to reach the safety of shelters around the mine before the blasts took place.

Andrew Parker and Dick Wilson used to arrange to be together at blasting time, undercover, but within throwing distance of Aubrey's office. Counting the siren down to within a second of the actual blast the two offenders would have selected pieces of rock as ammunition for their dastardly deed. As soon as the blast occurred they would hurl their rocks at the side of Aubrey's office, with the ability of seeing his reaction when their rocks hit the target.

Although rocks from the blast had hit the stores in the past, it was more likely to be the ones from our two jokers which caused Aubrey to leave his office to go to remonstrate with the pit manager for causing damage to his stores. The manager had no alternative than take all the blame especially when confronted with the rocks as evidence.

De Beers employee caught stealing diamonds from the old style grease tables.

Security suspected a reduction plant employee was stealing diamonds but needed to catch the man with diamonds on him.

Unbeknown to the employees, the grease tables section of the plant, the final recovery area, was modified by the installation of special observation walkways in the roof and one way mirrors which enabled security to have 24 hours surveillance at this crucial point. This was at the time when the most trusted workers were allowed to scrape off the diamonds on the grease tables with a scraper and gloved hands, which enabled the selection of the majority of special diamonds before they went into the final phase of sorting after the tables.

The security observers, using binoculars, noticed unusual movements of one employee when sorting, when he frequently moved one finger of the glove onto an oncoming diamond instead of using the tweezers allocated for the task.

When they searched the suspect for diamonds, after he had left the sorting table, they found several diamonds in the palm of his hand and on checking the gloves, found that one glove finger had a hole in it which had enabled the man to work the stone up into his hand and from there to his pocket. He was sacked from his job and taken to court where he received a sentence of 18 months.

The security procedure is much different today since my friend and I were both thoroughly searched before we were allowed to leave the mine on our visit 25 March 2008.

One piece of good news appeared in the De Beers News from the Mines magazines whilst we were at Lime Acres with a heading of 'Passing the Buck To Finsch'.

Since their establishment in pioneering days, diamond mines have kept and bred indigenous game, and in more leisurely years of the past De Beers maintained huge herds of blesbok and springbok on their vast outlying properties, complete with full-time keepers, comfortable and well-stocked shooting boxes, special shooting-brake vehicles and all other paraphernalia appropriate to the hunt or annual cull.

To conform with the tradition of game conservation Finsch Mine asked Jagers to supply sufficient blesbok stock to form a nucleus of a herd at Lime Acres. Accordingly a smooth wire game trap was built, a zoological game expert hired for the occasion, and under the direction of Jagers Security Officer the drive started in cold weather.

Initially time-consuming, arduous, wearying and frustrating work fell upon the mounted drovers and two African riders who drove the herd into the trap. Once past the entrance to the trap, two employees made their appearance from the rear of the herd, and so assisted in driving them into the trap.

Sixteen buck were caught and crated in special crates provided by the Zoological Gardens, Bloemfontein. All except one buck arrived safely in Finsch.

On Friday 28 August 1970 Jim Burgess and I left Finsch Mine at lunch time for Kimberley to see a rugby match in Port Elizabeth at the invitation of Huisey Huisamen and his friend Bokkie Norden. The game was Springboks versus New Zealand and by 2.30pm we were on our way for the long journey. Our hosts were certainly good entertainment and as the beer flowed we all opened up with our rugby stories and songs as well. Both Bokkie and Huisie had experience at provincial rugby level and the stories never stopped. This was apart from every 100 miles or so when we wanted a pee, Bokkie would set the empty cans up on a road-sign in the form of a pyramid just to show other rugby supporters we had passed that way.

By the time we arrived at the hotel for our overnight stay, I was well away (plastered). I had hardly recovered by the time we set off next morning for the match at the Boet Erasmus Stadium, which was the home of the Eastern Province RFU.

Before the match, the All Blacks executed their ancient tribal war dance the 'Hakka'. I found it a spectacular and stirring event and even now, I still get a shiver of excitement when I see it being performed.

As with the earlier game at Bloemfontein against France, the match was another cracker with the Springboks beating New Zealand 14 points to 3. The scorers for South Africa were left wing Gert Muller 2 tries, full back Ian McCallum 1 conversion, 2 penalties and for New Zealand 1 penalty. The attendance was 55,000. We were all very tired on our way back home, with far less drinking involved, but it had been a trip to remember.

One of the final spectacles for the family at Lime Acres occurred with a Soap Box Derby which was arranged by the Round Tablers. This proved a wonderful outlet to the up and coming young "speed fiends". The long steep hill down from the mine was used as the speed track and the various home-built carts demonstrated the wide variety of design capabilities among the mining fraternity. A special race for fathers and mothers was the last event, leaving hardly any carts left over for the following year's race.

My transfer back to Kimberley was organised in late 1970 after I had been invited by the De Beers Assistant General Manager (AGM) Hubert Wright to visit the O'Kiep copper mine, in what was then SW Africa to have a look into their usage of computers for the monitoring and control of the grades and volumes of copper ore.

It was quite a party of us who flew in the De Beers jet aircraft from Kimberley to O'Kiep situated near Springbok in SW Africa which apart from the AGM included our Chief Engineer Owen Parnell, my ultimate boss at the time.

I hadn't been briefed as to why I was in the party but found out half way through the tour of the mine when Mr Wright asked me if I had been taking notes. As a matter of fact I hadn't which meant I had to scurry back to the departments we had already visited to ensure I had enough data to create the report on our visit. My resulting report must have impressed the necessary judges because within a few weeks of the report being published I was invited to join a small team of four selected to set up the De Beers computer department from scratch. In the meantime, I was transferred from Finsch to Wesselton Mine as underground section engineer, as a stop-gap, while the plans to purchase and install the computer and ancillary equipment were developed.

Although I had enjoyed my time at Lime Acres I was looking forward to yet more new challenges. I doubt whether Iris, my wife, was as excited as I since it meant moving into abode number six in less than five years. And what about the children and their education? I hear you say. As far as I was concerned, when working for a company like De Beers you have to put the company first to retain and improve the rewards they pay for loyal service; especially when we were moving back to Kimberley, with all its advantages over Lime Acres, especially fresh milk for Julia.

Chapter Seven

Wesselton Mine, Kimberley, N Cape: December 1970

THE HISTORY OF WESSELTON MINE (extracts as described in the De Beers archives)

"WESSELTON DIAMOND MINE became established on what seemed to be a most improbable and unprepossessing site.

The farm 'Benaauwdheidsfontein', in Griqualand West, near Kimberley, was owned by Petrus Wessels and farmed by him and his foreman, Fabricus. Kimberley was growing rapidly from a camp to a busy town with a population of many thousands. Soon the town boundaries had reached the farm. Unfortunately, for Wessels, the rubbish of the town was dumped on the edge of his property. As these dumps began to spread he was forced to lease a large portion of his farm to the municipality for that purpose.

The piles of rotting and smouldering refuse, frequented by scavengers, made the farm an unsavoury place to be. Despite this, Wessels and his foreman went on trying to raise profitable crops. However, Wessels was worried about the state of his finances. There was a mortgage on his farm, held by Henry A. Ward, one of the Kimberley pioneers, who knew that diamonds could occur practically anywhere in Griqualand West.

Fabricus was asked to keep an eye open for diamonds although he knew that the farm had already been worked over by prospectors without success and a shaft had been sunk to considerable depth by Hermanus Prins without luck. 1890 was to mark the turning point in the farmer's fortunes. On a morning in September, Fabricus spotted a pebble that seemed different from the others. It was a diamond. Before that day was over everyone in the Kimberley area seemed to know that diamonds had been found among the rubbish pits.

Apparently the farm foreman had struck it rich by doing something which, according to the text books, could not lead to profit. He had dug through ground which the expert would have claimed as unpayable. Yet 10 feet below that mass of limestone lay the familiar yellow ground, which was all too well-known to the diamond diggers. Only two months after Fabricus had picked up that little stone it was proved that this area was certainly rich in diamonds. Geological investigation showed that the shaft Prins had sunk was only about 100 yards from the edge of the true diamond pipe.

Before the discovery of diamonds in Griqualand West that area was considered to be part of the Republic of the Orange Free State. It is certain that the Cape authorities did not dispute the authenticity of the title deeds issued from Bloemfontein. Under these title deeds the owner of a farm was also the owner of all mineral rights on his property. This law was different from that of the Cape, which reserved certain mineral rights to the Crown and attached various conditions to others. One of the farmers who held such a title deed was Petrus Wessels. Wessels was in an interesting position. Even before it was decided that Griqualand West should become part of Cape Colony it had been found that the boundaries of the colony had run through his farm. When the whole of the farm fell within the Cape area, attention had to be paid to the fact that the old Orange Free Sate title deeds were still valid. All this did not matter much when Wessels's farm was in the process of becoming one big rubbish dump, but it was a different matter when diamonds were found there. That title deed was to be a source of much litigation. It was to be years before all disputes were finally settled.

Naturally, Wessels was now in a much better position. He was ready to sell the farm for £175,000. Ward was interested, but the feeling among Kimberley business men was cautious and it did not seem that any of them would be willing to advance so large a sum. They saw other difficulties ahead. The farm was now crowded with a disorderly mass of diggers, who had rushed on to the scene soon after the news had got about. They would worry if Ward held out that by buying the farm he would acquire the sole right to prospect and dig. The matter soon went to law, and then the question of those obscure title deeds had to be considered.

Ward had to fight these lawsuits and he lacked the money to do so. In a desperate effort to raise funds for this purpose he had to sell a half share in his holding for £3,000.

This £3,000 share was soon purchased by De Beers Consolidated Mines for no less than £120,000. This led to another of the lawsuits around the Wesselton Mine, which was then known as the Premier Mine. Ward contested the legality of the investment before the Chief Justice, Sir Henry de Villiers, in the Supreme Court, Cape Town, and lost the action. De Beers was named joint owners with him. In the meantime Ward was still owing the £175,000 he had paid for the farm, and the date on which his option was due was drawing nearer. Ward was certainly a keen and persistent man, and even now was not beaten. He came to an arrangement with the heirs of Petrus Wessels under which, instead of paying them the original price, he would pay them £300,000, provided there was a considerable extension of his option. De Beers advanced the price rather than lose the mine.

Cecil Rhodes was interested in Wesselton from the time the first reports were made confirming the richness of the area. Only a year after Fabricus had picked up that stone, Barney Barnato was able to tell De Beers shareholders that the company had a 50 per cent participation in the new big diamond enterprise being launched outside Kimberley. That mine was known as Premier Mine, a name it was to hold for several years. The name Wesselton Mine was substituted when the Premier Mine in the Transvaal came into existence.

Some time before this, a final agreement was reached between Ward and De Beers. In the terms of this agreement, the ownership of the mine was to pass entirely into the hands of De Beers on January 11, 1896, but in the meantime Ward was to have the sole right of working the property.

The agreement provided that Ward could treat a maximum of 5,000,000 loads, or 4,000,000 tons, of the diamondiferous yellow ground. Various factors were taken into consideration relating to land area and depth of unpayable limestone. The farm, which was eventually purchased for £303,000, covered an area of about 52,000 acres. Ward had to repay his share of £151,500 out of his earnings. He was able to raise a loan to erect a mechanical washing plant to treat up to 5,000 loads a day, yielding a daily average of 800 carats. It was estimated that before the agreement expired in 1896 Ward recovered well over 1,000,000 carats, and these were sold at an average price of 18 shillings per carat. Most of this huge sum was profit, however, for the working expenses only totalled £82,500.

Under the terms of the agreement the whole of the property reverted to the corporation. It was then planned to carry on with the mining operations on much the same scale as those maintained by Ward. In fact, to the men working there the day Mr. Ward finished and on which De Beers took over were very much alike. The same routine went on, even though the employer was different. The men who gathered round to shake the hand of Mr Ward and wish him well need not have envied their "lucky" employer for, as events turned out, he was not as shrewd with his investments as he was with his bargaining.

Wesselton Mine, discovered in September, 1870, has yielded over 67,000,000 tons of blue ground since it   first commenced operations and from this ground over 18,551,860 carats of diamonds have been recovered (these figures applied in 1954). The mine was noted for its fine pure white diamonds."

I was appointed section engineer at Wesselton Mine with effect from 11 January 1971 but moved back to Kimberley just before Christmas 1970. One of the benefits for the children was that they could attend the Christmas tree festivities in Kimberley, which were larger than the event at Lime Acres.

Father Christmas staged his arrival at De Beers Stadium for the annual children's Christmas tree and party in a vintage car (he must have borrowed one of Kobus Van Jaarsveld's cars) and a larger than ever crowd of little people welcomed him. General Manager Ken Loftus welcomed everyone and was accompanied by senior officials of the company and their wives. Entertainment included a display by De Beers dogs, a conjuror, the Kimberley Regiment pipe band and rides for all.

As in previous moves, there was no engineer's house available to us at the time of the move so we had to make do with temporary accommodation until a new house had been built for us (as it happened it was on the same street, just four doors away). The first house was a reasonable size and quite adequate but paled into insignificance when we moved to the new building which I will describe later.

One of the first things I did was to join De Beers Country Club (DBCC) bowls section in Cassandra. It was quite an impressive setup with a large club house and two greens, one equipped with floodlights for evening play. This meant the members could play evening sessions throughout the year if required. Strangely enough, most of the people using this facility proved to be blind bowlers, trained by volunteers from the club. First the bowls coach positioned the bowls mat for the blind bowler so the bowler could feel the position of the mat which helped him to position his feet in the right direction. Then the coach placed the jack some distance away from the mat in the centre of the rink and shouted to the blind person the distance he had to throw his wood. This helped the blind bowler to know which direction he had to play and the distance he had to deliver the wood. The main drawback to these events was the large tin shades fitted over the floodlights. In the gathering dusk the light spilled down so that it was like daylight on the green. This resulted in hundreds of moths and flying insects spinning and dancing under the lights; tiny planets orbiting erratically around four extremely bright lights. This didn't really distract from the blind bowlers' enjoyment of their game of bowls!

Now that I had decided that bowls was my sport, I chose to invest in a new set of woods. I went to the main sports supplier in Kimberley, 'Kent Sports', to buy my bowls. After handling a number of woods for weight and bias I decided on Slazenger 5 inch heavyweight, which I still play with. Slazenger withdrew from the bowls market some years ago so I am now the owner of a rare set of woods, quite antique as they go.

As the engineer in charge of the mine I was pleasantly surprised to find a bowling green in the African hostel grounds. Although it was only of a three rink size and was little used by the African workers during their leisure time, I enjoyed the facility most lunch-times to give me practice with my new woods and delivery. I have always tried to follow the old saying 'practice makes perfect' and in my case that is exactly what happened. In my first season I surprised everyone, including myself, by winning the DBCC 'Men's Singles' title at my first attempt. I am confident that the main reason was my practising on the Wesselton green. I beat my best friend and coach, Rodger Symcox, in the final, the day before we left to go on our holidays to the UK.

One of the bowling club members, Harry Sadler, owned a jewellery shop in town. He offered me a good deal on mounting Iris's diamond, bought through De Beers, on a gold ring, setting the stone in platinum. We had to make a visit to choose the ring and to measure its size from Iris's finger. One evening, a week later, Iris had her belated solitaire diamond ring celebrated in style at the Country Club.

Early in 1971, on our way to take a short holiday in the Kruger National park, we visited our friends, Mike and Elaine, who had left Welkom to join AAC at Sallies Gold Mine near Springs, Johannesburg. After leaving Mike and Elaine we set off in the car for the Eastern Transvaal, spending most of the day driving, until we reached the park, checking into a rest camp before night fell.

The Kruger was the largest game reserve in South Africa. It covered 7,332 sq miles and extends 217 miles from north to south and 37 miles from east to west, approximately the size of Wales. The park itself had been in existence since the early 1900s. It was virtually unrivalled in species diversity, both animal and plants. Figures indicated that there were over 100 species of mammal, 500 species of bird, and nearly 2,000 plant species in the park. At any given moment there are thought to be around 8,000 elephant, 1,500 lion, 1,900 white rhino, 220 black rhino, 15,000 buffalo and up to 900 leopard in the park.

We arrived in Southern Kruger via the busiest entry point, Paul Kruger Gate, the nearest for Skukuza Camp 310 miles from Johannesburg. We entered into an area encompassing about a fifth of the Kruger National Park, and located between the Crocodile River in the South, the park's border and the Sabie River. Skukuza was the biggest camp and the park administration centre and perfect for the first-time visitor. It was situated on the junction of the Sabie and N'waswitshaka Rivers, providing some of the best drives in the park. Skukuza is a Shangaan word meaning 'he who sweeps clean.' We were advised that, although there was usually heavy tourist traffic, we had probably the best chance of seeing, in the shortest time, the "big five"; lion, leopard, elephant, rhino and buffalo and a variety of other game.

The entrance to the camp was dominated by a mini-escarpment marking the drainage area of the Sabie River. More water means more animal and plant life can be supported. The trees in the Sabie catchment area were bigger, the bush denser and more diverse and animal and bird life was very strong.

The closer we got to Skukuza, the more variety of animals there was to be seen. Initially, the vegetation was quite thick, but as the thorn thickets thinned out, there was more open grassland where large herds of grazing animals and predators could be found.

All we needed was a night's rest and some refreshment and Skukuza was ideal. The camp was a game-fenced area on the river bank where the cottages with circular walls stood under wild fig trees. These structures, peculiar to South Africa, were known as rondavels. They were thatched with a rough-hewn timber roofing and compressed earth floors covered with cured animal skins and rugs. As night fell, the air became soft and we heard a haunting bird call before we drifted off to an uneasy sleep in our rondavel for the night.

We enjoyed a camp breakfast before setting off for our next anticipated lodging at Lower Sabie, approximately 50 miles away. A short while into our trip we saw a lion with a large mane lying underneath the trees in the shade. He got to his feet and casually looked upwards, then seemed to shrug his shoulders and to flop down again with an air of intense boredom. We still expected the warden to come round to deliver carcasses for them at set times as they do in a zoo. For the next three hours we drove towards our destination and saw a wide variety of game, including elephants eating their breakfast from trees.

On arrival at Lower Sabie we received the disturbing news that all their accommodation was fully booked. The manager advised us that it would probably be the same at all other locations and said we would have to leave the park by closing time at 6.00pm. What a disappointment. We had no alternative but to head for the nearest exit to the south. I chose the Crocodile Bridge gate which would at least give us sight of different terrain and animals than what we had experienced on our way in.

As we moved out to the south, the Malelane Mountains could be seen and we also saw the Lebombo Mountain Range over the game-dense grasslands to the east. In the open were herds of game. Impala, twisting and leaping away at the first approach; kudu, with big ears and soft eyes; black sable antelope, with white bellies and curved horns and zebra, trotting like fat ponies. The going was easy and, occasionally we pushed to keep our speed up. Suddenly, turning out of a 90 degree bend, I pulled the car to a tyre-squealing halt in front of two exceedingly large giraffe, just managing to avoid an accident with one of the giraffe in our attempt to get out of the park in a rush.

The giraffes were bent towards small spreading acacia trees, their strange, stilt-borne bodies and their patch-work necks camouflaged among the leaves. We regarded each other with curiosity. Of all nature's odd creations, I think the giraffe is among the oddest. I felt as if we were being observed by a genial lighthouse and for a brief second I looked almost straight into the liquid eyes of the nearest one. It was staring at us over the top of the tree with an expression composed equally of intense alarm and immense curiosity. It finally loped away from us with a stately gait, no doubt a relief to all of us.

We journeyed on, getting hotter and hotter, and more and more irritable with having to travel at 30 mph instead of the normal 10 mph in order to ensure we arrived at our destination before closing time. At last we reached the Crocodile Bridge exit to the park at just before the deadline of 6.00pm

We had come to the Kruger because it was one of the last places on earth where wild animals exist in anything like their natural state. The great herds and migrations are gone, but the park managers have given its residents the freedom of an extremely large wilderness. For the most part it was savannah bush veld, rolling plains covered with dull-coloured bush and relieved here and there by craggy koppies. It was a deceptive landscape, seemingly empty and yet teeming with life. The wildlife we saw was formidable and I think we were lucky enough to see three of the 'big five' - lion, elephant and buffalo - during our time in the park, which was restricted to just one and half days. What an adventure to tell our grandchildren in years to come!

After leaving the park we found ourselves taking part once more in a dreary battle for accommodation. Fortunately we saw a small motel near Barberton, just before it got dark. We were all so shattered that it took very little to get us off to sleep, even in new surroundings and new beds. I was so tired that as I pulled alongside the hut allocated to us I caught the veranda upright with the car's front panel, scraping off some of the paint. My first accident, after travelling for three years without any problems, apart from the breakdown between Bloemfontein and Jagers.

As was the norm in South Africa, most of the English boys had at some time or another suffered at the hands of one of the physically bigger Boers. Andrew kept mainly to himself, being initially rather shy plus being a Rooinek (Redneck or Englishman). He was also normally the smallest in the class, but if someone picked on him then he would always fight back no matter what their size. He was seen as being the one kid who had successfully fought back and won. Hence he acquired a reputation and so was left pretty much alone by the bullies.

Other memories of Kimberley were mainly of the weather. In summer it would frequently get up to 40 degrees Centigrade and as the fierce afternoon sun beat down, the town and its residents baked in the heat. Whenever I got into my car I had to be careful that I didn't burn the back of my legs when wearing the mandatory pair of shorts or safari suit. The main relief was a visit to the DBCC to enjoy a few cold beers before returning home to the family.

In April 1971 I joined up with the Lime Acres bowls team

Elbie de Kock, Lyall Bennetto and Terry Freeme on our way to the National Bowls of South Africa Tournament to be held at Cape Town. Elbie, the GM of Northern Lime, drove us there in style in his luxurious Mercedes Benz company car which was just as well for it was a distance of 608 miles, which we achieved in a single day.

This proved to be a memorable trip especially since it was my first visit to one of the most beautiful cities in the world.

At the end of each day, after bowls and if I had the time, I would travel around the city to see the sights on offer. These were mainly centred around the bowling greens of Camps Bay, Fish Hoek, Green Point, Hout Bay and Muizenberg which provided a large rock pool for Capetonians to swim in and where Cecil Rhodes had died in his cottage in 1902.

One of the main sights I wanted to see was the Rhodes Memorial, built in his memory. The memorial situated above the University of Cape Town offered a splendid view of the city. It was built with granite extracted from Table Mountain and was surrounded by beautiful pine forests. Rhodes was not buried there; his body was transported by train and gun carriage to be buried in the Matopo Hills in present-day Zimbabwe.

Another was the Castle of Good Hope which was the oldest building in South Africa. It had the shape of a pentagon with five corner bulwarks and an almost 10 metre high wall formed from massive boulders. One of the views from it was of Robben Island where Nelson Mandela was incarcerated for 27 years.

Signal Hill's summit offered spectacular views of the city, the Twelve Apostles, the mountainous spine stretching south from Table Mountain and the ocean. Signal Hill's main tourist attraction was the battery with the Noon Gun positioned just below the mountain top. Here a cannon-shot was fired every day at 12 o'clock noon on the dot, to uphold an old Capetonian tradition.

Our performance at bowls was not as memorable. After we had been knocked out in the Fours competition I decided to return home by train and it was such a battle to get to the station it was hard to believe. I set off from the hotel to walk the 300 yards or so to the station but this proved difficult since the wind was blowing and it was one of the famous South Easters coming up from the Antarctic. The wind was blowing in gusts of more than 100 miles per hour and I was unfortunate to be carrying my suitcase.

I managed to get to within one street of the railway station when I found I couldn't get to the place from the corner of the building where I was attempting to cross. Every time I ventured out of the cover of the building the wind just blew me and my case back. After failing for 10 minutes to cross I had to think of an alternative plan of action, otherwise I would miss my train. I finally decided the only way of making it to the station was to attack the problem from a different direction. I accomplished this by going around the back of the building shielding me from the gale and that solved the problem since the wind then practically blew me across the road to the station entrance, just in time for the train to Kimberley. I was home late that night, disappointed with our bowls performance but glad to get away from the gale. It was confirmed later with reference to venues in the Bowls Magazine that on that day the wind blew so hard that games were moved from the Glen green to Pollsmoor & Oranjezicht because of the abnormal conditions.

All this took place while I was waiting for my next move in De Beers, this time into the world of computers and its myriad applications.

Chapter Eight

De Beers Computer Dept, Kimberley, N Cape: June 1971

W HAT WAS THE STATE OF COMPUTERISATION within De Beers in Kimberley in 1971? The answer was that the number of computers in place and the applications in operation was zero.

A notice from the General Manager of De Beers in June 1971 advised of the formation of a data processing department. The notice explained what the function of the new department would be and how the computer that was soon to be installed would be utilised. It attempted, briefly, to explain some of the reasons behind the new developments and what was hoped to be achieved (extracts are):

"1. What is Data Processing?

Simply stated, data processing is a series of planned actions and operations upon information to achieve a desired result.

2. Why choose a computer?

Computers came into being primarily to meet the increased need for information under increasingly complex conditions.

In September of last year a computer feasibility study was carried out in our Company. This proved that in the technical field alone the installation of a computer was justified. As an example one of the areas where "pay-offs" can be made is in mine planning. By using simulation and mathematical model building techniques coupled with the computer's fantastic speed numerous alternative schemes can be investigated for each new project, this leading to better decisions. Instead of being forced to implement one feasible solution done manually because of the lack of time to do others, the computer allows the best or optimum solution to be chosen. It is becoming increasingly expensive to be inaccurate and sometimes ruinous to be wrong. The margin for error nowadays is growing smaller all the time. As can be imagined the savings associated with the proper planning and timing of major mining projects can be immense.

However it is important to note that the use of computers does not lessen the need for executive decision making. Actually the reverse is true. But the manager is able to base his decision on much more current information and has faster and easier access to this information. Nevertheless people with knowledge and experience will always be required to put the information into the computer since the answers can never be better than the information put in the first place.

3. What is a computer?

The computer recommended for De Beers is the I.B.M. 1130.

INPUT: The input of coded programmes and data will be by means of punched cards.

PROCESSING: The control processing unit (C.P.U.) will be a model 1131 with 16000 "words" of core storage. (i.e. 16K of memory compared with 2 Gigabytes in today's laptop computers.)

OUTPUT; The main output device will be a model 1403 printer which is capable of printing 600 lines per minute. In certain cases the results of the process will be produced graphically on a plotter.

4. What will the computer do for us? This question has already been partly answered and the field of applications is immense. In the technical area applications include mine planning, production planning, ore reserve calculations, sampling results, geological forecasting, surveying and ventilation calculations, engineering planned maintenance etc. However, even to implement

some of the above-mentioned applications is going to take time. Initially technical applications will be run in areas where it is thought the largest "pay-off" can be made. In this connection one of the first large programmes will be a mathematical model to simulate opencast mining. The "building" of this model is being undertaken by Mr Clive Wollaston who is a systems engineer from I.B.M. in Johannesburg. It is expected to take approximately 5 months.

In general a mathematical model is a method of simulating reality. The model, simulating real life can determine the most profitable decision beforehand. Simulation turns hindsight into foresight. It minimises risk and removes much of the expensive error from historical trial-and-error methods.

5. Where is the computer?

The data processing department will be housed on the ground floor of the Consolidated Buildings. Work is presently in hand on turning the old Board Room into the Computer Room. When it is all completed we will have the finest computer room in the country - a combination of old and new, complete with stained-glass window, vaulted roof, teak panelling and bookcases!

As for the D.P. Staff it was decided that because of our basically technical applications it would be better to train experienced mining men to program the computer than vice versa."

This was confirmed by the release of the computer team's major players whose background was as follows:

THE DE BEERS COMPUTER TEAM - Robert McCallum, Jack Beal, Denton Tee, Len Thompson.

Robert McCallum B.Sc. (Mining Engineering), Superintendent of Technical Services, was born in Kimberley and attended Kimberley Boys' High School before joining the Company as an official learner in 1954. In 1966 he was appointed as mine manager. In 1970 he had acted as Assistant General Manager and in December 1970 he graduated from the programme for Management Development of the Harvard University Graduate School of Business

Administration.

John Elvy Beal was appointed section engineer at Bultfontein and Dutoitspan Mines in July 1964 and was elected a corporate member of the IMechE in that year. In May 1969 he assumed duty as the section engineer at De Beers Mine.

Denton Tee worked under Bob Dowie in the De Beers Benefit Society, Pensions Fund and Provident Fund Department. Denton was put in charge of computer operations responsible for the punch card, verifying and computer operations. One of the encouraging signs against apartheid was that two well-educated coloureds were employed in the computer operations department and they both provided an excellent service throughout the time I was involved with technical services.

I was appointed as technical systems analyst, reporting directly to Robert. My responsibilities were primarily the development of the computerised optimum open pit modelling system but also to assist with the development of Data Processing Standards and Procedures for the department. I was fortunate enough to carry with me the same benefits as my previous position as underground engineer e.g. 6 weeks' annual holiday.

As you can see, quite a powerful team to develop the computer systems and provide technical services to De Beers Consolidated Mines Limited.

The computer system was installed in Stockdale St Consolidated buildings just north of the De Beers head office. The old board room was converted into the computer room. One drawback to the room was the need for a large air conditioning system since, in those days, computers and heat didn't mix very well.

Our first need was to attend training classes at IBM's offices in Johannesburg. Robert, Jack, Denton and I spent two weeks there primarily learning programming languages such as Fortran and Assembler since there were no off-the-shelf programmes such as Word, Excel, or Sage. We had to develop our own computer programmes from scratch for our applications with the exception of the Open Pit Planning programme which was developed with the assistance of IBM's Clive Wollaston.

While undergoing the computer language courses I had a chance to discover Johannesburg in greater depth. The high plateau on which Johannesburg was built was originally an arid place inhabited by a few Boer farmers grazing cattle and cultivating maize and wheat. This harsh and isolated landscape was transformed after the discovery of gold in 1886. The mines expanded as new technologies opened up the deeper deposits of gold and Johannesburg was gradually transformed from being a gold rush boom town to being a large, modern industrial city but still known as the city of gold.

Johannesburg was now the largest financial, commercial and industrial centre in South Africa. The city was just over 80 years old and, since the gold rush, had grown into one of the wealthiest cities of the world. Settlers from all over the world had been arriving in Johannesburg since the first weeks of the gold rush, including people of Eastern European, British and African descent. At one time, this mixture of cultures produced a vibrant cosmopolitan atmosphere, but Apartheid changed all that, creating deep divisions in society that remain evident today. Most white residents lived in the attractive and affluent northern suburbs whilst the black African population lived in racially segregated, planned settlements on the outskirts of cities, known as townships. These areas tended to be some distance from the city centre and were divided from the white suburbs by areas of unoccupied land. There were often only one or two access routes into the township and the streets were originally wide and straight. Both factors were deliberately intended to make the control of unrest and protest easier to handle. The best known of these township areas was the vast residential area called Soweto, which originally stood for South Western Townships, on the outskirts of Johannesburg, which had been at the centre of the unrest reported in chapter two.

153

The vibrancy was still there during the day but with the 9.00 pm curfew in operation it certainly dimmed after that time. That doesn't mean to say we had much night-life since our training courses were extremely demanding and most of the time we were doing revision or homework to keep up with the course tutors.

The main highlights to me of any free time during the Johannesburg visit was the newly built Carlton Centre Complex which was the biggest project of its type constructed in South Africa. It was also the tallest building in the southern hemisphere when completed and is still apparently the tallest building in Africa. There was an observation deck on the top floor giving a bird's eye view of the city of Johannesburg.

As far as shopping was concerned, I favoured African art and curios which were of widely varying quality as many were imported from other African countries. I found sculptures, baskets, ceramics and beadwork extremely good value that made excellent souvenirs for our return to the UK or as birthday or Christmas presents. Wirework sculptures and African jewellery also made good presents, with the added bonus of being light to carry home. Johannesburg, with its big shopping malls, was also one of the best places to seek out designer bargains, as well as slightly cheaper versions of international brands.

After completion of our training Bob Dowie, a director of De Beers Benefit Society, Pensions Fund and Provident Fund and the President of the S African Bowling Association, asked me if it was possible to develop a computerised draw for the National Bowls Tournament to be held in Durban in 1972. Computerisation was required because of the complications of large numbers of entries in to the tournament e.g. 2216 bowlers for the fours competition and 2475 for the singles. Their names were required to be drawn randomly into sections with the minimal possibility of clubs or players from the same area playing each other. We managed to perfect a program.

The result of our development is logged in the South African Bowling Championships Tournament Official Handbook 1973.

"LEN THOMPSON - Pioneer of the Computer Draw

In early June 1971 I was approached by Bob Dowie, President of the South African Bowling Association, with the suggestion that the draw for the National Tournament, to be held in Durban, be done on a computer. He said that at this stage, in view of the adverse comments, all discussion and plans were to be treated as confidential.

Plans were made to arrange for a bowls draw which would cater for either Fours or Singles with variable numbers of entries and sections. This was complicated further as it was necessary to ensure that there would be no more than one club from a particular district in any one section, provided of course that there were fewer clubs from a district than there were sections. The difficulties really arose when I realised that Southern Transvaal and Natal would each have sufficient entries to necessitate two and even three fours in each section.

A major difficulty confronting the designs of a computer system is to have the job requirements specified clearly. Then considerable time is saved when it comes to programme testing as most, if not all, of the system faults will be brought to light.

Since this was to be the first computerised draw, the design approach was based upon analysing the manual method of breaking it down into its basic elements. These basic elements were translated into computer instructions with editing controls built in to minimise and correct inaccuracies in transferring data to and from the computer.

There were many snags and problems, all of which were successfully ironed out. My greatest regret is that, with a big machine now installed, I am unable to proceed further to perfect a system which I inaugurated.

Achieving the objective was made possible only by the help and guidance given by Bob Dowie and his Executive who, apart from

155

defining the job requirements, also assisted in designing the computer input documents and output reports.

It proved to be a very rewarding experience for me as I was able to participate in producing the first computer draw. I trust that the work we accomplished will be a boost for the game that has provided us with so much pleasure."

I have since developed an improved version of the random draw program which runs via the Internet at www.sportsdraw.co.uk for knockout league competitions and tournaments.

Iris and I had agreed prior to emigration from the UK that we would only be away from home for five years. However, since I had just started my computer career with De Beers I was able to convince Iris that it made sense to return to South Africa for two more years and she agreed to do so. My argument was that with another two years' experience in computer applications I would be able to enhance my prospects of getting a job back in the UK, either as a mechanical engineer with mining experience or as a computer applications engineer. This proved to be correct since I certainly had difficulty in 1973 trying to obtain a job as a mechanical engineer on any of the UK mines available in those days, whereas jobs in the computer field were much easier to acquire.

On 22 June 1971 we left South Africa for the UK for a three month holiday out of six months' long leave which I had accumulated out of my annual six weeks entitlement working with AAC and De Beers since 1966. I was able to cash three months of the long leave to pay for the holiday under their generous holiday policy.

However, it also meant I had to forego a visit to Nchanga mine in Zambia to look at their computer systems involved in the monitoring and control of their copper mines; which I had really been anticipating. I had already obtained my visa and authorisation to go. What a pity I couldn't have done both.

Chapter Nine

Long leave holiday in United Kingdom:June 1971

THERE WAS A BIG DIFFERENCE between our trip to South Africa in 1966 and this one to the UK. The previous one to Johannesburg had been accompanied by apprehension; not knowing what sort of life and conditions we were to face. Our return journey was supported by five years' experience of a new way of life, our family love, and a new member of our family Julia to show off to everyone we met back home in England. Waiting there would be our family and friends, who we had not seen for a long time.

I had learnt from our mistakes five years previously when flying from Heathrow to Johannesburg and ensured our return via BOAC was a shorter and quicker journey with just one stop at Entebbe airport in Kampala, Uganda, in both directions.

We set off for the UK from Jan Smuts airport on 29 June 1971 on a BOAC Boeing 707 (or, possibly. the latest 747-100 recently added to their fleet.)

On arrival at our stop at Entebbe I stepped out of the plane on my own while Iris stayed on board with the children since I did not think it was safe for them to leave. Being near the equator the heat and humidity were stifling as the sun bounced off the tarmac. General Idi Amin headed a country still very unsettled after he had come to power in a military coup on 25 January 1971. Amin had led the coup while President Milton Obote, the man who led Uganda to independence in 1962, was out of the country attending the Commonwealth conference in Singapore.

The coup in Uganda was just six months old and Amin would go on presiding for another seven years. Kampala, the capital city, was the administrative, political, commercial, industrial, educational and cultural centre of Uganda. The city had an area of 190 km2 and is 8 km north of Lake Victoria (the second largest fresh water lake in the world) and approximately 42 km north of the equator. I did not have to venture far to get a glimpse of what lay in store for anyone intent on making trouble. All around the airstrip were tanks placed at strategic positions and Ugandan soldiers armed with automatic weapons. I had a cup of tea and returned to the aircraft.

When we arrived at Heathrow, Iris's mum, dad, grandma Whittingham and brother Eric were there to meet us with a mini-bus big enough to carry us all and our cases plus presents for the family and friends. However, my brother Bob was also there in his car so I went with him while Iris and our children went in the mini-bus. The main attraction to both of our families was obviously Julia since only Sandra and Iris's mum had seen her in the flesh during their visit in 1968.

My first port of call was to see my mam and dad as soon as possible after being away from them for five years. Iris, naturally, went to stay at her parents' house 10 miles away.

One of the presents I had brought for my dad was some dried biltong which I was sure would give him a real taste of South Africa. Dad was used to unusual dishes such as eels, either from the sea or freshwater, and such delicacies (to him alone in the family) as pig's trotters and cow's udder. When I gave dad the biltong he asked what it was and whether he should plant it. I suggested he try the black strips of dried salt meat for supper and wash it down with a drink of beer. After looking at it for some time and finally tasting it he said he still preferred the planting idea.

Iris and I had discussed what we would prefer to do while we were in the UK and we had decided to have a seaside holiday with our closest families. After giving my mam her presents from Africa I then discussed the possibility of our going on holiday. We decided on a week in Cornwall. Mam said she was looking forward to babysitting the children while Iris and I enjoyed a bit of night-life on our own. We settled on the quiet little Cornish gem of Crantock Bay since we were told it was perfect for families seeking a relaxed holiday. I booked a caravan for us on the Crantock Beach Holiday Park overlooking the sea and a wide sandy beach. There were miles of coastal paths to explore during the day and in the evening we could sit outside a nearby pub and drink in the atmosphere of the quaint village.

The next step was to organise a hire car for a period of three months since, in those days, no one had a spare one that we could borrow. Our close family was still not so well off as to be able to do that. With the assistance of brother Bob I managed to arrive at a good deal for that period and I then had wheels for the duration.

After a few days spent mainly with Mam I went to Iris's parents' house to show them the car and discuss similar arrangements for a seaside holiday with them. Their preference was a holiday at the Derbyshire Miners' Holiday Centre since Iris's dad, as a coal miner, received a big discount on the normal cost of holidays there. Lots of his friends also went there, making it a home-from-home atmosphere for him.

My son Andrew certainly enjoyed himself in the UK. He went daily to the local shop for his supply of Milky Bars and developed almost an addiction to them, so much so he was called the Milky Bar Kid in Chesterfield. He would not eat other sweets and on one occasion when the shop had run out of Milky Bars he refused another kind instead.

The main problem we had with him and, to a lesser extent, Leon was not wearing shoes when playing outside, something natural for them to do in South Africa but against the grain in England.

Julia was ill part of the time with high temperatures and Iris's mum was advised by a friend to bathe her in lavender water to get her temperature down, which worked. She still had to go to see mum's doctor, who provided Julia with other medicines to get her through her ailments during our visit.

Our journey of more than 320 miles from Chesterfield to our first holiday in Crantock was of little challenge to a driver familiar with South Africa roads. Leon commented that it was rather strange not having dirt roads in England, nor the extremely long, straight roads, as far as the eye can see, to which we were accustomed in the OFS or Northern Cape provinces. Cornwall with its many inlets and coves plus the beach at Crantock Bay was a joy to behold. The beach itself was extremely long, wide and spotlessly clean, washed yellow by the sea and bleached white in parts by the sun. Most of the time we spent on those sands and the boys really lapped it up; as shown in the accompanying photo showing Andrew covered up to his neck in sand after being overpowered by 'Pirates Leon and me'. The bay also provided good waves for them to surf on, a skill they had developed at various resorts in South Africa.

The second holiday with the Stones family was quite different. We stayed for a week on full board in the miners' holiday-camp in Skegness. We had frequently been to Skegness before our children came along and it was only 85 miles from Chesterfield. The main benefit to us was the holiday-camp atmosphere for the whole family. There were always things to do during the day such as donkey rides on the sands for the children followed by treasure hunts and sandcastle competitions on the beach. When the sun was shining Leon and Andrew made straight for the outdoor swimming pool where they could demonstrate their swimming and diving skills.

During the day and evening there was a good compere in the theatre organising such things as talent shows followed by fancy dress competitions for the kids and knobbly knees competitions for the mums and dads. One fantastic bit of fun for the kids was on the polished ballroom floor, where they all took off their shoes and, with just socks on, ran their hearts out slipping and sliding around. When fine we could all go for walks along the sea front and the wide, decorative boulevards of Skegness. When raining, the children could always play in the covered amusement park.

Iris's dad had always enjoyed himself there ever since a stay at the camp's convalescence home while recovering from a severe back injury he had received down the pit. We even had a game of bowls on the camp's bowling green, where I was able to display my new-found skills.

Iris really enjoyed being in the company of her mum and dad, who were also willing babysitters. That gave us the freedom we hadn't experienced since moving to South Africa and the opportunity to visit many of our old haunts, pubs, clubs and cinemas as well as many visits to friends and family. I also called on my numerous cousins in and around Chesterfield and had pleasant times talking about South Africa and what we had seen and done while we were out there. We would also discuss the benefits and faults of that country, primarily to assuage their fears for us returning to a country which hardly ever got a good press in England.

My dad had retired from work but still had a keen interest in 'going to the dogs' since he was still shown great respect for his knowledge of anything to do with greyhounds and always had punters pestering him for tips at the various meetings he went to.

The overall visit, however, proved to be a disappointment to me. Iris and, especially, the children enjoyed the spoiling by their grandparents and close family but there was less enjoyment for me when looking back at my time spent with families and friends. I was now a misfit in their way of life. They had a settled existence, with due importance attached to various happenings that were no longer my way of life. For example, I was on holiday and they still followed their normal routine. My sport was now bowls and there were very few bowls clubs in Chesterfield. Those that were in existence only played crown green bowls, whereas we played on flat greens in South Africa. I now preferred rugby but my friends and family still supported their football teams. Even the drinking of beer differed since I was now a lager drinker and my friends drank beer. In other words, I now represented a way of life outside their circle of interests and I was a different person from the one they had previously known.

One of the main objectives to our trip to the UK was to decide if we could live here again, assuming that we would return to England in two years' time as Iris and I had agreed just prior to this holiday. By spending three months 'Back in Blighty', we felt that at least we had proved that Iris and the children would be able to settle back in the UK with little difficulty provided they could count on the support of her family. I wasn't too sure about myself.

Our final act was a shopping trip to obtain presents for our close friends, which were either hard to get, unobtainable or banned in South Africa, such as girly magazines like Playboy or Penthouse, for my pal Rodger.

On 24 September we arrived back in Johannesburg and apprehensively made our way slowly over the tarmac to the terminal building. On entering the block we were confronted by an official waving his arms to get our attention. We were on South African soil, he announced, which meant we had to clear immigration. We followed the line of passengers and when our turn came, I handed in our passports. In that cold, automaton manner so characteristic of white South African officialdom, the immigration officer checked our details and pointed towards the customs hall. We finally made it through the passport checks and into the baggage hall and then to customs where we had to obtain clearance for our cases and bags.

A customs officer spoke first in Afrikaans and then in English with a guttural tone. He had a voice like ice, aloof and superior. He then made me open one of my bags. Iris had packed most of them so I wasn't sure which one contained the 'banned' magazines destined for Rodger. He emptied a load of books and shook the bag, examining it for hidden pockets then checked the seams. His dedication was admirable. I gave a huge sigh of relief when we all found that they were not in that bag and we were told to go through to the green light passageway.

After the three months in England I returned to Kimberley, feeling disoriented and dazed by what we had just been through. Having seen our families after such a long time away made Iris even more determined to return in the two years I had promised. Myself, I wasn't too sure. Since so much had happened to us in South Africa in such a relatively short space of time, when looking back, I felt I needed to stop, take stock of what had happened and think through, logically, what the near future held for all of us. During our time in SA there had been very little time to do that. I must confess that, at that moment in time, I was in two minds, recognising the differences between the two alternatives, De Beers with its fantastic present and, no doubt, future opportunities and the UK, really an unknown quantity. However, I had made the promises to return to Iris and my mam and intended to stick to them unless there were dramatic changes in our circumstances.

Chapter Ten

Return to De Beers Computer Department: September 1971 to September 1973

O N OUR RETURN from the trip to the UK, I was immediately thrown into the development cauldron of the open pit planning system (OPP) with Clive Wollaston and the national bowls tournament draw with Bob Dowie.

Clive was finalising his design and programming of the OPP system. This kept me busy testing the 22 system programs and 27 function sub-routines (smaller programs). In between this testing I was working on the development of the bowls program, mostly in my own time, including weekends.

The basic problem in starting a mine, as in any other business, is: Will it make a profit? This is a formidable question due to cost escalations over a 30 to 50 years' life. Will the ore yield enough value to pay for the whole project and provide an acceptable rate of interest on the capital invested?

To show how difficult it was to answer that question we had to look at the variables involved. The aim of the OPP mine system was to provide the answers far quicker and more accurately than by using manual calculations. The variables were:

1)   Geological - rock types to be mined. Accurate dimensions of the diamond pipe were required to calculate the amount of ore and waste rock to be removed, using contours of the pipe at small degree intervals, bench widths, slope angle, stripping

ratios etc

2)   Financial - capital and working costs, taxes, loan levy etc.

3)   Production - production rates in rock and ore stripping using different earthmoving equipment at varying costs etc.

4)   Diamond factors - diamond grades per ton, per cent gem content, revenue per carat, stockpiling effect, gem sales, industrial diamond sales etc.

The OPP system was able to help by calculating the break-even point for the depth of mine when the workings would change from open pit to underground. It also assisted with forecasting and planning which were paramount for successful management and in those days of large surface mining enterprises employing expensive machinery in mechanised production, planning assumed even greater importance.

As you can imagine the computer helped tremendously with the speed and accuracy with which calculations were done. But one point which, for me, stood out was that sound judgment was still one of the main factors. We always bore in mind that the human element was still a very important factor in all of our undertakings. That is why it was the correct policy to have a top mining man at the head of our department.

The concentration of diamond in kimberlite, capable of economic exploitation, was of the order of only 1 part in 15 million parts by weight. Although the diamond content was often used as a rough measure of profitability it was the value of the diamonds that was the overriding factor. The value of an individual good diamond may be two hundred times that of another diamond of the same size. Not only do the individual groups of diamonds vary greatly in value, but the range in value of individual stones is such that a single good quality diamond of moderate size may change the aspect of profitability of any part of the mine.

Before the final decision to embark on a new venture was taken its investment potential was assessed. A typical example was the Letseng le Terai project for Lesotho where I was involved in using the OPP model system to ascertain its potential.

If my memory serves me correctly, the system arrived at a return of 17% on the capital employed and the decision was taken by De Beers to invest in the mine in partnership with the Lesotho government.

By coincidence Jim Burgess, who I had worked with in Kimberley and at Finsch mine, was the mine engineer during the construction of the Letseng mine.

Unfortunately Jim was killed in a motor accident in August 1981.

THE HISTORY OF DIAMOND MINING IN LESOTHO

"Lesotho is an enclave within the Republic of South Africa. Popularly known as 'The Mountain Kingdom' it was, until 1966, the British Protectorate of Basutoland, It is 30,000 sq km (11,600 sq miles) in area (approximately the size of Belgium) with a population of 1.8 million (2006).

For many years the Basotho workers had provided the diamond mines at Kimberley with much of their labour force and, thus, were well acquainted with diamonds and 'blueground'. Once back in their own country they put this knowledge to good use. In the late 1950s kimberlite pipes were found at a point known as Letseng-la-Terai, the 'turn by the swamp'. In 1955 Colonel Jack Scott, a colourful veteran of the South African mining scene, received a licence to prospect the whole country for diamonds. However, confronted by ever-increasing demands on his personal resources without expectation of an early return, Colonel Scott in 1959 entered into an agreement with De Beers who undertook to assist him with the prospecting programme.

The terrain of South Africa is mostly continuously sun-drenched but Lesotho is mountainous and the diamondiferous areas lie more than 9800 feet (3000 metres) above sea level and are exposed to every permutation of the elements - wind, sun, rain, cloud, hail, sleet, frost and snow. Thus a combination of an awkward and remote geographical location and an inhospitable climate rendered working conditions very difficult and frequently hazardous. For these reasons and because the diamondiferous area appeared to be too low in grade for exploitation, De Beers withdrew from the scene in 1960.

The government at once set about establishing a public digging at Letseng-la-Terai. Claims 10 feet (3 metres) square were pegged out over the whole area of the pipe and were offered to Basotho at the rate of 50 cents per month for each claim.

The early recovery of some fine quality diamonds exceeding 50 carats stirred up interest. Foreign diggers, bringing with them finance and skill gained from experience of the South African diggings, entered into partnerships with the local diggers. In addition, buyers, principally from South Africa, appeared, setting up offices and appointing representatives in Maseru, the capital of Lesotho. The buyers usually visited Maseru twice a month to buy from the diggers who made the long trip down from the mountain to the capital on foot or on pony. Some of the buyers used to fly up to the diggings once a month, using the air strip for light aircraft that had been constructed on the top of a hill.

The method of mining was primitive but effective. In October 1965 a stone weighing 527 carats was found by a 67-year old digger who promptly fled to the hills, saying he feared for his life. The great moment of discovery, however, took place on Friday, 26 May 1967, when a brown stone weighing 601.26 carats was found. This was the 'Lesotho' diamond which ranks as the eleventh largest of gem quality in the world.

Moreover it is the largest ever to have been discovered by a woman, Mrs Ernestine Rama-boa, the wife of a 38-year-old digger,

Petrus Ramaboa, of Thabana-Morena. Since the start of their digging the Ramaboas had experienced reasonable luck, finding several stones including one of 24 carats. Petrus Ramaboa decided to walk the 225km (140 miles) to sell them. Whilst he was away his wife came upon the big diamond. Without a word to her fellow diggers she departed to her hut to await her husband's return. When he saw it he decided they should set off at once for Maseru, The couple walked for four days and nights. News of the find spread rapidly among the buyers in Maseru and eventually the government stepped in for the Ramaboas' own protection. A meeting was arranged between the Minister of Economic Development, Senator C. D. Molapo, and representatives of the registered diamond-buying firms for discussion on the government's procedure for selling the diamond. Dealers were shown the diamond and were requested to submit sealed tenders. The highest bid of R216,000 (£108,000) was from a Bloemfontein dealer, Eugene Sarafini.

In the late 1960s production at Letseng-la-Terai started to decline. In 1976 the country's ruler, Chief Jonathan, asked Harry Oppenheimer whether De Beers might conduct yet a further evaluation of the Letseng-la-Terai deposit.

De Beers agreed to proceed. In November 1977 a modern mine was officially opened. Sadly its life was destined to be short. The Letseng-la-Terai deposit proved to be one of the lowest grade diamond mines in the world producing only three carats per ton. It also yielded an exceptional number of large stones: in the space of five year. It produced more than 100 diamonds weighing more than 100 carats, including one of 213 carats. However, due to the depressed state of the diamond market in the early 1980s, particularly for the larger, high-quality stones produced there, the mine had been operating at a loss for some time and was closed."

However, conditions in the diamond market did improve. In 2004, four flawless diamonds weighing between 72 and 112 carats and worth about £3.2m were discovered within six days in the

Letseng mine, which De Beers had abandoned.

In September 2007 Gem Diamonds Limited announced the recovery of a 494 carat diamond from the mine. This remarkable diamond is believed to rank as the 18th largest rough diamond. The Letseng mine, which is 70% owned by Gem Diamonds and 30% owned by the Government of the Kingdom of Lesotho, has produced two more of the world's top twenty diamonds: the 603 carat Lesotho Promise recovered in August 2006 and the Lesotho Brown diamond recovered in 1961.

Letseng also produced a 215 carat D-colour flawless diamond in January 2007. The Letseng Mine hosts two kimberlites; the Main and Satellite Pipes that have a combined diamond resource value of US$4.7 billion. It is renowned for producing some of the world's largest diamonds which attract the highest average price per carat of any kimberlite mine.

During November 1971 I flew to CDM on the far west coast of South Africa to attend a high-powered course on advanced statistics. This was to prove extremely useful in the next six months for my investigations into diamond ore grades and gem content of the open-cast mines at Finsch and Koffiefontein.

Following the course I did analysis work on Finsch mine and demonstrated my new found expertise by producing an equation from graphs of gem content against depth of pipe that gems would disappear at a certain level. Robert McCallum invited me to discuss my findings with Mr Ogilvy Thompson the CEO at AAC while he was on a visit to Head Office. He was extremely interested in the work.

Dave Rankin, our Divisional GM was, however, rather disturbed, since Robert hadn't cleared it through him.

The national bowls draw was run on Saturday 20 December 1971 on the IBM 1130 and was a complete success as can be seen from an article in the Diamond Fields Advertiser (DFA) on Monday 22 December 1971.

BOWLS DRAW BUTTONED UP

"Automation came to sport in a big way on Saturday, when the draw for the 65th South Africa men's bowling championships was made in Kimberley.

For the first time in the history of bowls in South Africa, the new draw was successfully done by computer - a system which heralds a new era in sports administration.

This year 554 fours teams, 2475 men's singles and 391 veteran's singles entries have been received - a record - and the entire draw, from the moment Councillor GH Venter pressed the button to set the Diamond Producers' Association computer in motion, took just under an hour.

In the past the draw for the championships took a group of workers an entire day to complete, and Mr Bob Dowie, president of the South African Bowling Association, which is based in Kimberley, said yesterday that the system of doing the draw manually was 'dead forever.'

Once the draw had been done, it became the DFA's job to transmit a copy of the computer list to other news sources in South Africa. An indication of the amount of work involved can be drawn from the fact that the newspaper's telex operator took four hours to put the draw over the line.

The copy of the draw, which appears in today's paper, took a Linotype operator close on two hours to set in print.

Among the dignitaries who attended the meeting were Mrs Ruth Keytel, president of the South African Women's Bowling Association, Mr Andy Young, Mr Eddie Pepper, tournament chairman and secretary respectively for the championships which will be held in Durban.

One of the key figures in bringing about the computerised draw is Len Thompson of De Beers, who played a large part in programming the cards that were fed into the machine."

The actual draw took place on the IBM 1130 computer in the De Beers Consolidated Building in the presence of the Mayor of Kimberley, the full South African Bowling Association executive committee and guests. The draw was available to the press within the hour and everyone, especially me, heaved a huge sigh of relief.

The De Beers Christmas Tree event for 1971 was held on the fields of the De Beers Country Club. Once again the weather was unkind and due to the high wind the display of model aircraft had to be cancelled. The two clowns in their beach buggy caused much merriment while the Pipe Band heralded the approach of Father Christmas in his jet aircraft.

The highlight for the children was a diamond rush event. The person who staked the right claim was awarded a prize. In addition there was a period costume contest.

Since our return from the UK, Leon and Andrew kept asking when we would get a replacement for their former pet Alsatian, Bruce. Iris and I decided to get them a dog and we spotted one for sale in the DFA at a farm on the way to Riverton. While they were at school I took Julia with me and she chose the one she preferred and that was the job done. This time it was a Welsh terrier, which we naturally called Taffy. He was covered in fleas, but after delousing and de-fleaing, he was loved by the whole family and by our African assistants. Taffy proved to be extremely skilled and fearless and no doubt responsible for killing a snake that Julia remembers seeing laid out on our back stoep when she was still a little girl.

In my 1972 diary I have an entry that we took Taffy, aged 3 months, to a private vet for a 3 in 1 vaccination which included rabies. After that, Taffy was always healthy until the time Leon was playfully fighting with him and caught poor Taffy on his eyeball with his fingernail. This caused the eye to swell to twice its normal size because the eye duct was apparently blocked but we still loved Taffy, no matter how he looked.

On Sundays, just before I went off to play bowls, I always took him out for his early morning walk around the DBCC cricket ground. This was probably the best cricket venue in South Africa, even having an electronic scoreboard, well before any other cricket club in the country. De Beers always looked after their sportsmen and there were plenty of them.

Besides Taffy, there were white mice for Leon, Andrew and Julia to play with. We had bought Leon a tame white 'mickey' mouse from the pet shop but, lo and behold, it turned into a 'minnie', suddenly producing several babies. We never did get to know where the father came from.

We had taken one white mouse, in its cage, to Durban with us in the car in the winter of 1972 when I represented DBCC in the SABA national bowls tournament. Unfortunately I was in charge of it when Iris and the children returned to Kimberley by air and I forgot all about it for 24 hours. In the heat of Durban it died within that time with no food, drink or even a car window open. I felt guilty for weeks after and apologised to Leon most profusely for my neglect of his pet.

I kept myself amused at home by making biltong and hanging it up in the store room to dry, only for it to go missing. No doubt one of the boyfriends of our maid Flora must have seen or smelt it. That sort of luxury was a temptation to anyone, black or white.

That reminds me of another of son Andrew's escapades, this time with a 'Tokoloshi'. It is an African spirit, more of a devil really, that strikes the fear of God into African women. Well somehow he got hold of a small black wooden statue of a Tokoloshi which came from our trip to Swaziland. So with his statue in hand and mischief on his mind he would creep into Flora Matwetwe's small quarters and hide under the bed and then jump out when she came into the room, brandishing his Tokoloshi. Her reaction was to jump on the bed, scold him seriously and shout 'Go away naughty boy' or something to that effect. She later told him that was why African women have their beds on bricks, raised up, so the evil Tokoloshi can not get them and do whatever it did!

In February 1972 Robert McCallum, our Superintendent of Technical Services was transferred to Western Holdings in Welkom to join David Rankin, formerly Assistant General Manager, Districts, at this mine. His replacement was Andrew Peter Brittz, a De Beers man, big, in all senses.

Andrew was appointed as the manager of the department. He was born at Keetmanshoop, South West Africa, where his father was a native commissioner. He started his schooling at Sidney-on-Vaal and completed his studies at the Christian Brothers' College in Kimberley. He joined the company in 1944 at Jagersfontein in the survey department. He became a learner official and was subsequently appointed a shiftboss. He was transferred to Kimberley in a similar capacity in 1952. He obtained his mine overseer's certificate in 1953 and was appointed a mine overseer in 1956. He obtained his mine manager's certificate in 1961 and returned to Jagersfontein as underground manager.

In 1962 he was appointed manager of Wesselton Mine, and in 1966 was transferred to Bultfontein Mine as manager. He had acted as assistant general manager for long periods. He was certainly a heavyweight who was able to keep our technical services department in the forefront of the company.

Within a few weeks of meeting Andrew he offered me the use of his holiday home at Gonubie, just north of East London on the Eastern Cape coast. Iris and I decided to take advantage of a week's holiday at the first opportunity of school holidays, since we could not afford to take the children out of school any more after their three months in England.

So we set off for the drive to East London which was not too far at 410 miles (750 kms). The trip was a pleasant one, through Bloemfontein, Aliwal North, Queenstown and Cathcart. This time we took our maid, Flora Matwetwe, with us, primarily to look after the children, especially Julia. We passed through the Drakensberg mountains and the nearer we got to our destination the deeper the valleys and dales became. As we approached the coast, East London loomed out of the mist and rain, a dreary port sprawling around the mouth of the Buffalo River. We then drove 12 miles northeast and came into Gonubie, the resort overlooking the Gonubie River and a lagoon plus a beach promenade leading to the wilderness of huge sand dunes.

Leon remembers the following:

"Going on holiday to Gonubie or Umhlanga Rocks but I think the former, one summer probably around 1971/72 and playing on the most amazing beaches. There were these massive big sand dunes that Andrew and I used to roll down, until we found an old car bonnet. We dragged that to the top of the dunes, sat in it and pushed off and what a ride: all the way to the bottom and then the long haul back to the top. It may be that the tide came part the way up at one point and we flew down into the waves on that car bonnet, but I'm not sure. I think on the same holiday we found a dead shark about 3 feet long and dragged it all the way up to the car park. We knocked on the car door and mum opened it up and I asked if we could take it back home with us? I think she went mad. There used to be some rocks on the right hand side of the beach where you could watch sharks swimming and we watched in amazement as divers dived in and swam with them. There was also a whale calving out in the bay and we tried to swim out to it but couldn't get past the shark nets."

Gonubie was an extraordinary area of sand dunes and dune forest facing the sea. The highest dune rose just over 250m above sea level. The forests were inhabited by vervet monkeys, bushbuck, and numerous forest birds. There was also a small picnic site, popular with local visitors who came there to fish and surf.

I remember sliding down the side of the dunes with Leon and Andrew, the fine sand making a growl as it cascaded like liquid ahead of our feet. I have stood atop dunes in the UK but none anywhere near the size of those at Gonubie.

We would then walk down to the beach, feeling the sand soft beneath our feet. Just beyond reach of the white foaming arcs spilling across the sand we stood mesmerised at the beauty of it all. Then Leon and Andrew would swim and catch fish with hand lines in the rock pools and play war games in the sand dunes.

We observed a whale with its baby either at Morgan's Bay or the mouth of the Kei River, both north of Gonubie, which we visited on our way back home. Perfect resorts for a peaceful beach break and a taste of the Transkei, an area of outstanding beauty, designated for some of the Bantu homelands. The countryside looked beautiful with green, rolling hills dotted with rondavels - round thatched huts - but as I turned off the main highway on to the Queenstown road I was ready for home in Kimberley.

In June 1972, with just over a year before we were due to leave South Africa, we all made a visit to see Johannesburg and Pretoria. On our way back we decided to call and see Gerald and Pam Price and family, who had been transferred to Witbank Colliery. We stayed overnight at the Casa Mia hotel in Johannesburg to enable Iris and the children to see the mining and financial capital and the main shopping malls. Having already been around the city it was a relief for me to get out of Johannesburg and I felt my spirits rise as we headed north on the freeway towards Pretoria.

As we climbed the low range of hills above the city we looked down on Pretoria. The jacaranda trees that filled most gardens were in bloom - masses of purple - and the busy streets typified the prosperity of the Transvaal province. Our main objective was a distinctive landmark still dominated the approach to South Africa's capital from the south.

The Voortrekker Monument stood on the top of a hill, a huge granite cube commemorating the epic expedition of thousands of Afrikaners who quit the British Cape colony in the 1830s in search of land and freedom.

Over the years the Great Trek has been romantically portrayed as an exodus of biblical proportions, although only a fraction of Dutch-speaking settlers in the Cape joined the wagon trains heading north. Yet it was a momentous migration, similar to the settlement of the American West which took place about the same time, and for many Afrikaners it was a cornerstone of their culture.

Die Groot Trek was the stuff that legends are made of. In the space of six years about 15,000 Afrikaaners struggled over mountains and deserts, braving drought, flash floods, malarial mosquitoes and hostile natives who were understandably reluctant to hand over their lands to the newcomers. Killing and looting were the order of the day, with the spoils of land and cheap labour going to the men with guns and Bibles. The indomitable spirit of the voortrekkers is depicted above the entrance to the monument in the sculpted head of a buffalo, which is reputed to be the most unpredictable and dangerous animal in Africa, particularly when wounded. It was a stark mausoleum with a high domed roof, and in the middle a granite tomb commemorating those who died in the trek was illuminated by natural light softened by yellow mosaic windows. Around the walls was a bas-relief depicting scenes of life on the trail: ox-wagons departing from the Cape, battles with natives, making peace with natives, more battles with natives, crossing mountains, and so on.

The most dramatic frieze depicted the Battle of Blood River in 1838, when a punitive expedition of 470 Boers under the command of Andries Pretorius defeated an army of more than 10,000 Zulus. This was taken as proof that God was not only on the Boers' side, but that he had given them a mandate to conquer and civilise southern Africa.

Hence the Day of the Vow, (or Covenant) to honour God and carry out His work.

From the roof of the monument there was a fine view of the city named after the victor of Blood River, nestling in a green valley framed by low hills. A prominent feature was the red roofs and sand-coloured facade of the Union Buildings, the seat of power from which ancestors of the trekboers administered the country for generations. The reason the government complex was still visible from the monument was that there are laws restricting the height of buildings to ensure that the view between the two was not obscured. Presumably the idea was to inspire the bureaucrats with the spirit of their forefathers, and to remind them that God was keeping an eye on them.

On our return from our trip up north I started playing bowls again at DBCC, where I linked up with Rodger.

Claude and Weston Symcox, Rodger's and Weston's dad, was Len Symcox and I was renamed in bowling circles as him so people called us the four Symcoxes. The four of us made a very strong combination, winning the majority of the games we played. For instance, we entered the Kimberley Open Easter tournament held at Beaconsfield Park, which attracted bowlers from afar. We finished up winning three seasons in succession but tired of the same prizes (sets of suitcases), so we finally resorted to giving them away to friends.

One of our most memorable games was played at the Ramblers Bowls Club in Bloemfontein, one scorching Sunday in 1972. This was an open tournament and the club was renowned for its generosity but they excelled themselves by their welcome. We were greeted by the most unusual sight. Just outside the clubhouse were three large tables covered with white linen and standing in the middle of each were bottles of whisky, jugs of ice and litres of milk. All the bowlers were told to help themselves and with it being so warm early in the morning we all got stuck in. Needless to say our opponents could not hold their liquor as well as we could and we scored an eight on first end (similar to a hole in one at golf). We went on to win the first prize.

We also entered the South African National Tournaments at Johannesburg and Durban representing the DBCC. Our most successful tournament was at Durban in 1972 when we won our section, consisting of twelve teams.

We succeeded in getting through to the last sixteen of the competition before being beaten by a side who had two former Springboks in their team. We also did well at the Johannesburg tournament held 13 to 26 May 1973 where we stayed at the Kelvin Grove Hotel. We only lost one game out of 11 to the winners of the section who came from Johannesburg and knew the greens far better than we did.

Our skip, Rodger, was the most complete bowler I had ever played with and even seen. He had the full array of bowls shots from excellent draw, no matter what length, to full blooded drive when taking out the opposition's woods from the head. His quality was confirmed when I visited South Africa on holiday in the late 1970s. By coincidence, the South African Masters Competition was held at Kimberley the same weekend and Rodger won the tournament quite easily.

One of the bowlers I met at DBCC was John Vanston, an immigrant from New Zealand, who introduced me to his wife, Barbara, a former New Zealand Olympic swimmer. This was an extremely fortunate meeting for Leon and Andrew since I was able to arrange swimming lessons for them with Barbara. We could not have asked for a better teacher. When we finally returned to the UK to live, they always beat the UK swimmers in their age group. On one occasion when Andrew was only nine years of age he entered three under-12 competitions, all against much older and bigger boys. The first two events he won easily. The third he won by at least half a length in a two length race, as far as I was concerned. However the judge disqualified him.

I asked the reason for failing him and the judge accused Andrew of standing up on the turn. I insisted on a rerun, which he again won by a half length. When the judge again disqualified him for so-called pulling himself along with the lane marker string I realised the judge was being totally dishonest. It turned out that the judge's son was in second position in the race. So ends the saying 'An Englishman is true to his word' or something similar.

Leon and Andrew were both at Herlear School in Kimberley in 1972. On checking their school reports my only comments are:

Leon's report contained a strange statistic in that he did better at Afrikaans recitation, oral, spelling and language with an average of 62% than he did at English with a score of only 46%. Does that mean MJ Storer, his teacher, was unable to teach his mother tongue as well as his new Afrikaans language?

Andrew's report shows he was industrious in class and did sound work. He was also obedient and helpful in class but should be encouraged more to do his homework, according to his teacher Miss FH Fothergill.

Leon and Andrews' final reports from Herlear School in September 1973 show that our decision to return to the UK had affected their schooling. Comments on Leon were: 'Leon has not worked at all well. I hope he will settle down and produce the sound work he is capable of at his new school.' E Chantler - Class teacher and HR Gaffley - Principal. Comments for Andrew: 'Andrew has shown a lack of interest in his work due to the impending move overseas, signed MI Watson - Class teacher and HR Gaffley - Principal. With all the disruptions both children had to put up with during our stay in South Africa there was no way we could complain at their performance.

More memories from Leon:

"The only one I can remember other than the obvious like Symcoxes, Wilsons and Lewins, is Robert Duncan who lived over the road in Cassandra and was called Carrot Tops because of his red hair. His father always drove a big Chevy-type car. We used to play a game called clay latte, which we named after the stick or latte in Afrikaans.

What you would do is get a load of clay, which we would dig

for as it had to be moist, and then get a latte about 3 feet in length. The end of the stick had to have a bit of bend or spring in it. We would then attach a large marble-size rolled piece of clay onto the top of the latte, and hold it out at the back of you at arm's length, and then swing it forward as fast as possible, which would result in the clay flying a good 50 to 75 metres at most.

We used to be able to control the distance and rough accuracy of the clay balls quite well. The trick was to apply it quite thoroughly to the end of the stick and let it stick for a 10 seconds and this would give the friction required to really catapult it. Anyway, we used to pelt people's houses with it. So someone would be sitting quietly in the front room and next thing half a dozen clay balls would pepper the windows and make a right mess. On one occasion we peppered the front of Carrot Top's house and his dad came flying out (which was quite scary as he was a big one-armed bloke). A few of us had let off another round and just as he came out he got a good sized clay ball which exploded all over his face. Well the cry that came out was one that would come from someone who could hardly see. This was fortunate for us as he couldn't really give chase so we legged it up the road laughing amid the torrent of abuse flying out from his garden."

In May 1972 a new computer system was requested by the Chief Engineer, Owen Parnell, and his request was passed to me for a response. The system was required to monitor and control all De Beers regulatory jobs daily, weekly, monthly and annually e.g. winding rope, boiler inspections etc. Although I could have written the specification for it I just didn't have the time, being fully engaged with the OPP system for both Finsch and Koffiefontein mines. I had no alternative but to ask for the specs to be supplied by the Divisional Engineer Len Wallace and advised him that no programming would be started until specifications were drawn up for the whole system. This didn't go down too well with my former colleagues.

Flora Matwetwe, the African woman who worked for us at

Cassandra, was one of the few housemaids that the whole family got on with. She was good at everything; ironing, cleaning and polishing floors and looking after the children, when needed.

We parked the Ford 17M in the garage and the mine car, under a carport just by the front door. By modern standards our bungalow was a large one, built for an engineer with status in the days when builders had no reason to worry about space. It was rather gloomy, with a corrugated iron roof. There were three bedrooms, one with an en-suite bathroom and a shower room which I welcomed after work in summer.

The floors were highly polished wood segments. Such floors always seemed cool in the hot months, encouraging the children not to wear shoes both inside and outside the house.

In Kimberley I found that the morning was the best time to address a problem. I was at my freshest in the first hours of the working day, when the sun was still low and the air fresh. That was the time to ask oneself the major questions; a time of clarity and reason, unencumbered by the heaviness and other factors of the day.

At the DBCC swimming baths, weekend after weekend, Leon and Andrew would show off with their friends, dive-bombing near the edge of the pool to drench the girls and do mildly difficult acrobatic tricks. A whole bunch of them enjoyed themselves in that fashion.

I can still remember the specialist's Dr Boardman kindly look, who assisted when we had to rush Julia into hospital with an extremely high temperature. He organised an ice bath which, thankfully, succeeded in reducing her temperature. It turned out that he was a close friend of Len Symcox who told us what he had said.

During one of our bowls matches I was approached by Jaapie Jooste, the president of the GWBA. He knew that I was the Match Secretary at DBCC and he asked me if I would like to join his committee as GWBA Match Secretary. I said I would consider it and discuss it with Iris. Iris agreed that I could take on the duties since, although Griqualand West probably covered a larger region than any other Bowling Association, there was a minimal amount of work due to the small number of clubs in the province.

At the next GWBA committee meeting, held at the men-only City Club in Kimberley, I was introduced by Jaapie to all his friends on the committee. They all extended their friendship as well as their assistance in helping me with the job. I was presented with a lovely bright clip-on tie and a smart wire-blazer badge which I always wore with pride when carrying out my association duties.

The first major problem I faced after joining the committee was a drinking one. I was a Castle lager drinker but soon found that I was outnumbered since all the rest were whisky drinkers, mainly White Label. As you can imagine, seasoned whisky drinkers could down two or three while I was drinking one lager.

I tried to keep up with them but finally submitted and changed to the majority choice of whisky. The next problem I found was that if I kept up with their pace I was having something like 10 or 12 tots and then having to drive home. The worrying fact was that I was able to, without even worrying about my ability to control the car. I was sure I wasn't affected but I probably was. Looking back I realise it was probably a good thing that we left South Africa when we did. Otherwise I could have had an accident similar to those that resulted in the loss of two of our dear friends, after we had left in 1973.

The 1972 Christmas tree event took place at the stadium on December 6, the last occasion on which this venue was used after well over half a century. Many hundreds of children poured into the grounds when the gates were opened at 3.30 pm. They were entertained lavishly until the arrival of Father Christmas later in the afternoon. Party packages containing sweets, hats, nuts and all that was necessary for a party were handed out at the same time as ice creams, cakes and cool drinks, whilst parents were entertained to tea. Before the ceremonial arrival of Father Christmas, in a moon-landing capsule complete with a section of the moon, there had been a display by De Beers dogs and a thrilling exhibition of karate. Culminating event of the afternoon was the distribution of presents, which were voted the best ever. A pop group band provided music for dancing and it was a tired but happy crowd which made its way homewards after a glorious afternoon of gaiety and fun.

Early in 1973 I was flown to Johannesburg, at the expense of Southern Transvaal Bowling Association, to give them advice on the computerised draw to be done for the following National Bowls Tournament, to be held in Johannesburg.

It was now nearing the time when we had to tell my employers and friends that we were leaving them to return to the UK: quite an unpleasant task that we had to perform.

Chapter Eleven

Resign from De Beers to return to UK: September 1973

I N SEPTEMBER 1973 it was officially announced that we were leaving De Beers and Kimberley with the following statement in the De Beers News: "Len Thompson, System Analyst, has resigned to return to the United Kingdom."

Just two months previously my company car had been replaced with a brand new 1.3 litre Chevrolet. Had someone in De Beers discovered that I was about to leave, to return to the UK? Was this their last throw of the dice to entice me to stay?

When I told my boss, Andrew Brittz, that I was really leaving, he offered me alternatives such as a position with AAC at an iron ore mine in Mauretania. The only employment I was prepared to accept was a job with AAC in London or with their engineering partner, Charter Consolidated, in the north-east of England.

In early September Iris decided what items she wanted to send back to the UK. I managed to put everything in our old wooden crates that we had retained since arriving in South Africa. A good job was found for our garden boy. Our maid, Flora Matwetwe, was given a handsome reward for all her hard work in helping us, especially in looking after Julia. She returned home to Kuruman to reflect upon her time with us. Taffy, our Welsh terrier, went to a good home just a few hundred yards above where we lived. We thought he would be ok because his new owners had a high wall encircling their back garden. However, we learned later that he practically pined to death. Any time that he escaped from the walled garden he would go straight to our house and sit outside waiting for us to return. An extremely sad ending to a faithful friend. All the furniture, apart from the small items we were returning to the UK, was sold in an auction that was attended by my coloured friends from work and a host of their friends. This was against the law but who cared at that stage? Not I. We had set up our braaivleis and the celebratory drinks flowed. It really was a farewell party.

We also had a party to end all parties for me with the attendance of all my closest friends Rodger and Weston Symcox, Ted Hall, Alex Lewin, Brian Ikin, Dave Renns (De Beers photographer) and Gordon von Mollendorf who I worked with in the computer department. The rugby songs, dirty stories from the magazines I had bought from the UK for Rodger and the drink flowed all night. At the end of the evening I was presented with another certificate designed by Ted, appropriately coloured, stamped and signed by my friends which stated in script lettering:

Competency Certificate

"This is to certify that Leonard Thompson after serving an apprenticeship of the prescribed period of 2 years, 8 months, 11 days under the tutorship of the undersigned, is now considered capable of drinking in any company. Certified by several signatories and dated 22-9-73."

There was some last-minute shopping that I had to do before leaving Kimberley. Firstly, I bought two small pure white diamonds (0.49 carats each), one for my mam and one for Iris's mum, from a Kimberley diamond dealer as my way of saying sorry for being away from home for seven years. Secondly, a bottle of whisky for my friend Dave Methven, to share with our GWBA colleagues. Their favourite tipple was White Label but I could only find a bottle of White Horse and decided to cover up the 'Horse' part with a printed 'Label' which caused some amusement among our friends when I presented it to him as my farewell gift.

The last days ticked away. Iris had already packed our suitcases with the assistance of Flora, carefully noting all advice about warm clothes.

As we left Kimberley for Cape Town on our return to the UK there were headlines in the De Beers News worth mentioning:

WORLD BOOM IN DIAMONDS

"De Beers Consolidated Mines is riding on the crest of a world boom in the diamond market, and came close to doubling its profits during the first six months of the year, raising net earnings by 58,5 per cent. The diamond market remains firm and there were three diamond price increases in the first half of the year and from the beginning of August there was a further overall increase of 10.2 per cent in rough gem prices."

So at least I was leaving the company in a very good financial state.

KIMBERLEY COLDER THAN ALASKA

"Kimberley, as residents know only too well, suffers extremes of climate. On the day a party of steam railway enthusiasts visited the city last month a man from Alaska announced categorically that it was far colder in Kimberley than Alaska." I told you it could get cold as well as hot in Kimberley.

MINE MANAGER COMPETES IN VETERAN CAR RALLY

"Dutoitspan and Bultfontein mine manager Mr D. J. 'Kobus' van Jaarsveld competed in the South African National Vintage and Veteran Car rally earlier this month. His entry was a 1924-type O.D. Vauxhall, the only one of its kind in South Africa. Kobus was accompanied by his wife Fienie who acted as navigator. The Van

Jaarsveld's car 'stable' includes an Austro Daimler, one of two surviving eight-cylinder cars of this make. The other is in a Paris museum."

As you see, our former friends from Jagers and Finsch were quite wealthy.

THOMPSON TROPHY FOR SERVICE

"At the annual meeting of the bowls section, held in the Country Club, Claude Symcox was re-elected chairman and Duncan Smith secretary.

The popular and efficient Len Thompson, who with his family will soon be leaving South Africa, thanked everyone for the wonderful times he had spent on the bowling greens of Kimberley, and as a token of his appreciation donated a trophy to the club, to be known as the Thompson Trophy. To his surprise, Claude Symcox was the first recipient of the trophy for outstanding service to the club during the past season."

So there is still a little bit of me out there in Kimberley.

A couple of items worth recording from May 1974:

AFTER A CENTURY - THE LARGEST

"THE largest diamond ever found in Kimberley was picked up on April 17 at the crusher station at Dutoitspan Mine to take its place as the ninth largest diamond in the world. The 616-carat yellow octahedron was found at Dutoitspan Mine on April 17 by 32-year-old Abel Maretela. This was Mr Maretela's fourth pickup, but the others were 'sugar grains' in comparison with the largest octahedron ever found. Wisely Mr Maretela banked a large portion of his reward and said that the discovery of the stone was 'just one of those things' and would make no difference to him.

One of the uses to which he will put his reward is in

educating his sons aged seven, three and five years.

Mr Maretela has worked for De Beers for 10 years and is one of four brothers with the company."

Even now some of the big ones are still there waiting to be found.

GINA THINKS HER PRESENT IS DIVINE

"The day before the largest stone ever found in Kimberley was picked up at Dutoitspan, the Sultry Italian film star Gina Lollobrigida had been underground at the mine.

The Diamond Fields Advertiser reported on the visit: 'Oooh la la! It's-a too magnificent, no?' The voice: Gina Lollobrigida. The sight: More than three million US dollars-worth of gems on display at Kimberley's famous diamond-sorting complex at Consolidated Buildings.

The famous Italian film star with the sultry looks and the flashing eyes winged her way into Kimberley to have a glimpse of the city's diamonds - and flew out with one in her possession, a sparkling octahedron diamond, set in matrix and presented to her by Mr Alex Hall, resident director of De Beers.

The presentation of the gift at a luncheon with senior De Beers officials and her viewing of the diamond-sorting were the features of her one-day visit to the city, during which she shot off reel upon reel of film in preparation for a photographic 'montage' of her stay in South Africa.

Filming is still very much part of La Lollo's life. But now she prefers to be on the other side of the camera lens. This was clearly evident as she clicked her way through a trip underground, a view of the sorting complex and a visit to the mine museum.

She was met at the Kimberley Airport after a flight from Johannesburg by Mr Alex Hall and was then escorted underground by the assistant general manager of De Beers, Mr Hubert Wright and the mine manager, Mr Paul du Toit.

Chief valuator Mr Mick Harris conducted her tour of the diamond sorting at Consolidated Building and then she was the guest of honour at a luncheon given by senior De Beers officers.

Fascinated at seeing diamonds in the rough, Gina has more than a passing acquaintance with the stones. Appropriately, she was wearing a magnificent blue-white stone of over 19 carats.

One aspect of Gina's trip underground she found rather disappointing. 'There's too much machinery down there . . . not enough men. For the industry perhaps this is good, for the photographer it is bad. She is not altogether happy about what is happening in the film industry. Too many of today's films bludgeon the public, she says, with sex, sensationalism and spectacle. Too few have the merit of being good stories.

'What about directing a film yourself?' she was asked. Pause. 'No, I do not think so,' she replied. 'I would have enough knowledge of technique and lighting and so on. But again there must be a film with a good story.' The next day Mr Hall received the following telex:

"Dear Mr Hall, again many thanks for your wonderful courtesy and hospitality. Your present is divine. Congratulations on your latest discovery of a 616 carat diamond. I hope I brought you lots of luck. Gina Lollobrigida." I am sure the luck flowed both ways but what an advert for both De Beers and La Lollo.

We travelled overnight by train, mainly passing through countryside I had seen before on my journey to and from Cape Town with my Lime Acres bowls colleagues when we had played in the bowls tournament. Finally, in the early morning light, there was Cape Town, cradled in a valley, the sprawl of skyscrapers, suburbs and shanties dwarfed by the might of Table Mountain. I realised this would become a dream for Iris and the children, seeing such a place of beauty whose sights would stay with them for a long, long time.

Leaving the train, who should we see but our friends the Lewins and the Halls who had planned the farewell surprise of seeing us off on the boat. Alex and Ted organised the rest of the day for us by taking us to all the sights in and around Cape Town, including a trip up Table Mountain on the aerial cableway.

Table Mountain, rising a sheer 1,073 m from the coastal plain, dominates almost every view of the city, its sharp slopes and level top making it one of the world's best-known city backdrops. For centuries, it was the first sight of Cape Town afforded to seafarers, its looming presence visible for hundreds of kilometres. Certainly, its size astonished us all, but it is the mountain's wilderness, bang in the middle of a bustling city, that makes the biggest impression. According to various statistics Table Mountain sustains over 1,400 species of flora, as well as baboons, dassies (large rodents) and countless birds. Much of the area is a nature reserve, and the mountain itself is protected as a national monument.

At the end of our quick tour I had difficulty thanking our friends for their gesture in coming to see us off. These were such fantastic people that they were obviously the major negative in leaving South Africa. We could never expect to replace such friends on our return to the UK.

However, I knew that fate would not let me down. I knew I'd be back and I told them I could hardly wait for the World Bowls Tournament which was due to be held in Johannesburg in 1976. It now certainly felt like the end of our journey but the enormity of what we had been able to achieve began to sweep over me as we prepared to leave.

I felt differently: I still couldn't quite take it in. South Africa had been unbelievable, complicated, and difficult. In some ways the place was so unjust; the poverty, the conflict, the hardship. Apartheid had shielded us from most of it. A lot had happened in the seven years we had been away from home and I had such a lot to think about. I had no real feeling of euphoria: just a sense of satisfaction, of a job well done both with Anglo and De Beers. During our trip on the liner back home to the UK I would have more time to reflect on our achievements and whether, looking at it from a personal point of view, we were doing the right thing. I now had plenty of time for reflection but, obviously, it was too late to change my mind.

We boarded the Pendennis Castle during the afternoon and our friends were allowed to join us to say 'au revoir'. During the day the farewell parties swarmed all over the deck. All around, the quay echoed the confused noises of music, laughter and sobbing. The water around the ship was so brightly lit it seemed there were lights below the surface. The deck was jammed with hundreds of people leaving and thousands who had come to see them off.

The liner sailed out of Cape Town on the evening of Wednesday 26 September 1973. The ship's maiden voyage had been in 1958. She was de-commissioned in 1980.

We were on our way back home to Chesterfield, Derbyshire. What ordeals would await us there? During the first few hours as we sailed into the huge swell of the Atlantic poor Iris went through the normal agonies of seasickness. Initially the voyage was too frightening for us to enjoy since Leon and Andrew needed constant watching every time they went near the ship's railings. The only times we could enjoy ourselves were when they dropped off to sleep. The romance of the voyage took charge on those occasions. After a week or so at sea, we would go outside, on top, where the air was soft and warm. Standing near the bridge of an ocean-going ship on a clear night, with the quiet roar of the waves in our ears, and watching the moon casting a silver path on the sea we sensed an utter detachment from the rest of the world. This was one of life's great experiences.

We remember playing deck quoits on board ship and of seeing flying fish and dolphins but most of our recollections were of the crossing the Equator ceremony. This consisted of pairs of people fighting with inflated plastic bags on a large greasy pole which had been placed over the swimming pool. Contestants were selected from those who had never witnessed the ceremony before. Each one had to get onto the pole, with difficulty because of the amount of grease on the pole, and then start hitting each other with their plastic bags until one of them slipped off and landed in the pool. The competition winner was awarded a prize by King Neptune, one of the ship's crew. All the losers were blindfolded and walked in front of King Neptune where eggs were smashed over their heads and then they were guided into a huge tub of mud, still blindfolded. The attendants dunked the men, but they were gentler on the women, just pouring mud over their heads. The blindfolds then came off and all losers had to pay homage to the court and kiss the King's belly.

Finally, they were allowed to go to the shower on the deck and watch the rest of the event. At the end, all those in the court and the attendants were bodily picked up and dunked in the mud. The contestants got their own back.

That night there was a fancy dress party. Leon dressed as a black ambulance man, of all things. This would have raised a few eyebrows among our Afrikaaner friends back in South Africa but it proved there was no racial attitude in my family.

Apart from the Equator ceremony the rest of the voyage was rather a bore for Iris and me. However the children lapped it up, especially with the swimming pool being so handy. They soon made friends and had a great time. The Pendennis Castle wasn't much of a ship. We didn't enjoy being trapped in a confined space with the children forever wanting to go out to play to release their boredom.

At least the ship did her job and got us back safe and sound to England. In the Bay of Biscay, on our last afternoon at sea, the ship ran into a gale, clumsily hurdling the enormous swell. By midnight we were in the Channel and we huddled together, out on deck, waiting to see the lights of Southampton. They materialised about an hour before dawn. There were just coloured lights and it was very cold. It had been a long time since I had been so cold. We went back down to our cabin, lay on our bunks, and wondered what would happen next.

What happened then is another story. The longer I have

stayed in England, the more numerous and powerful my memories of South Africa have grown. My recollections continue to return, especially on Sunday afternoon, typically when I am having a bath, the same time I would have been playing bowls for DBCC. I mainly imagine being on the green with Rodger & co. Because South Africa is so real in my recollection I can taste it and it tastes like happiness. At the same time I have never ceased to feel lucky - a lucky member of a hard-working generation. It is these memories and recollections of the marvellous places we saw during our stay in South Africa that helps to keep my dreams recurring.

Unfortunately these memories are tainted by the tragic deaths of two of our dear friends, after we left South Africa:

Arnold Lewin

Arnold was the son of our very good friends Alex and Jean Lewin. They travelled a distance of 1,216 miles (1,982 kms) to see us off at Cape Town when we returned to the UK via the Pendennis Castle. Jean came from Rugby in Warwickshire and Alex had met her when he was working in the UK. They also have a daughter Louise.

Arnold was born in Welkom on 20 November 1959, eighteen months older than Leon, but they played together regularly.

He started at Christian Brothers College, then on to Herlear School. When he reached standard 6 he showed potential towards engineering and so attended Kimberley Technical College. He soon showed much interest in his studies and joined De Beers as an apprentice fitter. He was successful as an apprentice and showed potential with his engineering skills.

Arnold was conscripted for National Service, which was compulsory by law, at the age of 18. His choice had been the Engineering Regiment but he was given the Signals Regiment and was stationed at Heidelberg in the Transvaal. He died, in suspicious circumstances, on 19 November 1978.

The following are extracts from newspapers, mainly from the DFA and Natal Mercury:

"A court case was brought against the South Africa Department of Defence at the instigation of Alex and Jean, who were not satisfied with the findings of the Chief State Pathologist that the cause of death was due to heat exhaustion. A second post mortem was carried out by a Kimberley pathologist, Dr B P Mather, who said that the possibility of a blow on the chest contributing to death could not be ruled out. The case was held in Windhoek between May and August 1979

Arnold had been sentenced to 14 days in Detention Barracks for allegedly being asleep on duty. He was examined by an army doctor at the barracks. Arnold told the doctor that he had gone for a swim and developed sore eyes from excess chlorine in the water. He had lain on the floor and put eye drops into his eyes. His commanding officer had found him lying on the floor with his eyes closed and accused him of sleeping on duty. The doctor considered Arnold a likeable person and felt sorry for him. He thought the sentence in detention barracks was harsh. Knowing how severe the exercises were, he had tried to find some medical reasons to put him on light duty but could find none.

The Windhoek Regional Magistrates' Court heard how Signalman Arnold Lewin entered the Grootfontein Detention Barracks on a Friday, was placed under intensive medical care after collapsing and died that weekend. Seven South African Defence Force members were charged with culpable homicide following his death on 19th November 1978. They were a Lieutenant, a Lance Corporal, four Riflemen and a Private. All entered not guilty pleas. One of the seven accused was dismissed by the judge before the trial started. The judge felt there was no relevant evidence against him. The case against the remaining six was initiated 'in camera'. Such proceedings can not be published.

The Court heard that, at 7.00 am, on the day before he died,

Signalman Lewin was in a group of about 20 prisoners who ran to an exercise ground and obstacle course about a kilometre from the barracks to start their day's physical training. They wore overalls and steel helmets and each man carried a rifle and a backpack, filled with gravel. Witnesses described the arduous nature of the exercises. These had consisted of jogging, press ups, sit ups, running with Land Rover tyres, heavy pole PT and gardening. Exercising groups that fell behind had to repeat exercises. If that happened members of the group might bump and trip the laggers.

A Sergeant Major agreed that the whole purpose of the detention barracks system was to make things as unpleasant as possible for the detainees to serve as a deterrent.

A witness stated that Signalman Lewin had complained of feeling unwell the previous evening. He was seen to stumble and fall several times and be unable to keep up with the other prisoners

Evidence was given that Signalman Lewin 'was hit on the back of the neck by a tyre thrown at him by a fellow prisoner...was punched in the mouth... was kicked in the ribs by a fellow prisoner during push-up exercises ... fell three to four times while running with a pole ... fell off an aerial apparatus ... collapsed while chopping at a tree stump at the end of the exercise period ... was hauled to his feet and jabbed in the chest by a fellow prisoner ... bounced up and down on the shoulder of another prisoner.' He collapsed a number of times. One witness said he felt the way Signalman Lewin had been treated was, 'to put it bluntly, inhuman'. 'You can drive a man to a point and no further,' he said.

After a final collapse he was loaded into a Land Rover and returned to his cell at about 9.30 am. A witness said he was thrown into the back of the truck like a shot kudu. Later he was seen in his cell 'covered with a blanket and staring at the ceiling.'

Signalman Lewin was admitted to the Grootfontein sick bay at about 12.10pm. He was draped with wet cloth, had cold water poured on him, his skin rubbed and given chilled replacement fluid intravenously He suffered a cardiac and respiratory arrest and was flown in an emergency mission to No 1 Military Hospital at Voortrekkerhoogte, Pretoria. He died the following day.

Professor Johann D. Loubser, Chief State Pathologist, said his finding, after doing an autopsy on the body and a microscopic examination of the internal organs, was that death was due to heat exhaustion.

Professor Loubser said that apart from multiple abrasions on the insides of both forearms and the knees, there was little else noticeable in the external appearance of the body. (There was no mention of bruises to the chest)

A second autopsy had been carried out at the request of the Lewins by Dr Brian Mather, a Kimberley pathologist and a member of South Africa's first heart transplant team. He told the Court that he found about 22 bruises on the body and limbs of Signalman Lewin, some up to 6.5 cm. He said Signalman Lewin died through bleeding into the lungs. He could not rule out the possibility that this was caused by a blunt blow to the chest but he added that one of the main causes of haemorrhage into the lungs was heat stroke. Dr Mather said his original finding that the pulmonary haemorrhage was due to 'blunt trauma to the chest,' was made in the absence of any background to the death and without clinical information.

Dr Loubser said, when told of a medical certificate declaring Signalman Lewin 'fit for detention' handed in as he entered detention barracks, that such a document was not license for one person to do with another what he wanted.

When Dr Mather's findings were put to Professor Loubser in cross examination, he replied that the discrepancies between his and Dr Mather's findings were not upsetting. He had viewed the body shortly after death and had a clinical examination. Dr Mather had done only an anatomical examination. Professor Loubser said he stood by his findings that the death was caused by heat exhaustion.

When asked about treatment for heatstroke, Professor

Loubser said the chances of survival and recuperation were critically short in time, even a matter of minutes. A person suffering from heat exhaustion should be treated when he showed the earliest symptoms, such as personality changes. It was important to spot why a person was slow to respond to command, why he was uncoordinated."

On the final day of the trial, held on 28 August 1979, the court's verdict on the six defendants was that two of the accused were cautioned and discharged after they had been found guilty of an assault on Arnold. The judge said 'the accused suffered enough punishment through the trial'. The remaining four were acquitted on charges of culpable homicide as well as alternative charges of assault.

Was this justice for the Lewin family? My own thoughts are that it was a terrible miscarriage of justice.

Alex and Jean Lewin were not satisfied with the outcome of the trial and, to this day, are profoundly saddened by the loss of their only son, a fine and worthy young man, on the threshold of life.

Warren Symcox

Warren Symcox, son of our good friends Weston and Sandra was just one year older than our Andrew and frequently played with Leon and Andrew and his brother Shane at Finsch mine and in Kimberley. Warren married Linda Hodgson on 8 December 1984 and they had two children Jaqui and Warwick.

Excerpts from an obituary written by De Beers for Warren are as follows: "26/02/1964 - 15/07/2002. Claude Warren Symcox was born in Kimberley on the 26th February 1964 and educated at Kimberley Boys High school where he excelled as a sportsman in cricket and squash, attaining colours for cricket in 1981. He was selected to play in the Nuffield Cricket Tournament in 1981 and was selected for the South African Nuffield side. He went on to play Griqualand West Cricket in the summer of 1984/1985 as a batsman.

From April 1987, Warren started a meteoric rise within De Beers working in London, Johannesburg, Antwerp, Hong Kong, Belgium and Israel, until returning to Southern Africa in 1998.

Warren was appointed as Diamond Consultant for Southern Africa in October 1999 and moved to Johannesburg with the responsibility for all liaisons of the Southern Africa offices and all South African rough diamond sales.

He was also a Director of DTC Valuations for South Africa, Namibia and BDVC, Botswana, as well as De Beers Angola Holdings.

In 2002 Warren was appointed as acting GM of H.O.H. in addition to his duties in Johannesburg. While serving in these posts, Warren was tragically killed in a motor accident on Monday 15th July 2002 while travelling back with family and friends after a weekend at a game lodge.

At the age of 38 Warren had achieved greatly in his career, on the sporting front and in his personal life.

He was a great asset to the DTC and will be sorely missed as a husband, as a father, a son, a colleague and a client, but most of all as a friend to all of us."

Just before Warren died, he became very interested in the many orphanages around Kimberley which were battling to make ends meet and he saw how tirelessly the staff worked without any complaints, their only interest that of the children who had either been orphaned by HIV Aids, or indeed, had the virus themselves.

Warren and wife Linda were based in Kimberley in the months prior to their accident. It was during the weeks leading up to his death that Warren and Linda spoke often about the orphans in Kimberley, which had obviously become important to him.

For this reason Linda decided to ask for donations in lieu of flowers at the time of his death. Her desire was to use the money for something he felt strongly about. The orphanage is called Sinothando and is based in one of the townships of Kimberley (Galeshewe).

Linda used the very generous amount of money to build an

attachment to an orphanage being built. Exactly one year after his death, on 15th July 2003, Jaqui, Warwick and Linda, with Warren's parents, Sandra, Weston and brother Shane present, opened the Warren Symcox Childhood Development Centre. The idea of the centre is to educate children in the area who are directly affected by HIV Aids. At present the centre educates 37 children every day and also provides them with three meals a day as well as other necessities such as clothing and bedding. These children are lucky enough to have a roof over their heads to go home to; unlike the babies who are housed in Sinothando, with the hope that they will be adopted.

It is my intention to help maintain the name of the Warren Symcox Childhood Development Centre by donating some of the profit of this book to Warren's Development Centre.

Tragic and untimely deaths such as I have recorded here have, in retrospect, fully justified our decision to return to the UK. Had we remained in South Africa our two sons would have had to serve in the army and, possibly, been subject to a brutal regime. South Africa is a country of dramatic contrasts, in terrain, cultures, climate and recreation. There is still that pioneering spirit that promotes risk-taking. By contrast, none of our friends in the UK have lost their lives.

On arrival at Southampton Docks a feeling of guilt surfaced at being away so long from family and friends. This was where our South African adventure ended.

Chapter Twelve

Conclusion

WAS IRIS CORRECT ON INSISTING that we return to the UK? Speaking as a family man I am sure she was right but I must admit it was a major personal wrench to me, leaving behind a job, friends and a lifestyle that I had grown to love. Probably the main reason she was right was that although South Africa was a beautiful country (God's own country as most South Africans used to say), it is also one of the most dangerous places in the world.

This was not the case when we were there since the whites were well protected, but over the years the safety aspect has deteriorated. To explain this I put forward the tragic deaths of four of our dear friends we had made during our seven years stay in South Africa. They were Ted Hall, Arnold Lewin, Jim Burgess and Warren Symcox (the deaths of the last three have been covered earlier).

Ted Hall. A very dear friend of ours who, with his family, saw us off in style when we left Cape Town to return to the UK.

TRAGIC AIR CRASH (Excerpt from the De Beers News July 1974)

"The chairman, board of directors and general manager of De Beers Company were among the first to express their sympathy with the families so tragically bereaved in the aircraft crash at Finsch on July 16.

Telegrams, telex messages and telephone calls of condolence from all over the world flooded into head office where personnel have been devastated by the tragedy.

Seconds after the twin-engined Beechcraft, Baron, piloted by chief-pilot Mr Piet Albertyn, took off from Lime Acres airstrip it was seen to plunge into the veld a few hundred metres away, killing all four occupants instantly.

There was a strong wind blowing at the time and an eye-witness account made to the police indicated that the aircraft banked to the left and then went into a dive.

Mr David Worthington, chief pilot for Anglo American was on the spot shortly after the accident where he told reporters that Mr Albertyn was a highly experienced pilot. Mr Worthington had trained Mr Albertyn 25 years ago under the SA Air Force scheme. Piet had over 12,000 hours flying time to his credit including experience on four-engined DC 4 aircraft."

Ted was one of the occupants.

"Edwin 'Ted' Hall was born in St Helen's, England in 1940 and was apprenticed as a draughtsman to the National Coal Board from 1956 to 1961 when he was made a junior engineering draughtsman. He served the board in this capacity until 1966.

In that year he accepted a position as engineering draughtsman with Crone & Taylor and in 1967 joined Pilkington Bros, in a similar position. He emigrated to South Africa in 1970.

He spent a year with General Mining & Finance Corporation as a draughtsman and approximately a year with an asbestos mining company as a design draughtsman. Ted came to De Beers on May 1, 1972 as a design draughtsman.

A jovial and lively personality endeared him to Kimberley's bowling fraternity who will also miss Ted as a competition secretary (he took over this position from me when I left in Sept 1973).

Prior to emigrating he married his wife Beryl from Rainford, St Helens, in Lancashire. The family consists of an eleven-year old daughter Susan, and a son Nigel who is seven.

At the time of going to press an inquiry team from the Department of Civil Aviation is investigating the accident. To the bereaved we extend our heartfelt sympathy."

Just to show what I lost when Ted died I include excerpts of some of his many letters to me, demonstrating his remarkable sense of humour and wit that enamoured him to "Hall and sundry" (as he would say):

Excerpts from letter 1 November 1973

"Dear Iris and Len, or Len and Iris if you prefer it, we were delighted to hear that you all enjoyed your voyage to the green, green grass of home. Is there any green grass in Chesterfield? I can't ever remember seeing any.

Thank you for your very informative letter, Iris; it was very well received by Hall and sundry. If I may be permitted one criticism, that is, you only managed to mention the master of the house once, when reporting that he had got all sorts of fancy ideas after watching 'Last Tango in Paris' at the local Bughouse, both Beryl and I were very surprised at your reaction Iris because we were under the impression that you were very experienced in that sort of thing. Maybe Beryl should have put you right on the facts of life before you left the virgin lands of South Africa.

To get back to your departure from Cape Town, please accept my apologies for my apparent lack of conversation during the final farewell, it is not easy to say farewell to someone who have been such wonderful friends to us in the short time that we have known you. The period of time may have been short but the memory will remain in our hearts for the rest of our lives, and both Beryl and I sincerely hope that we will be able to continue our close friendship with you despite the 6000 miles distance between us.

Please write to us regularly and keep us informed of your less personal activities particularly about the children. We will be really interested to know how they have settled down. Best wishes - Ted, Beryl, Susan and Nigel"

Letter 5 December 1973

"Dear Iris and Len

I cannot possibly compete with your magnificent piece of outstanding literature (your letter) you certainly seem to have many hidden talents Len; I was always led to believe that Iris was the letter writer in your family. Anyway be that as it may we were very pleased to get your letter and Beryl couldn't stop laughing while she read it.

Sorry Iris I know I addressed this letter to you as well, we hope your mink and knee length boots (and Len) are keeping you warm. Have a nice Xmas and think of us enjoying ourselves in the Terrace bar, I will write a more comprehensive letter soon.

Love and best wishes Ted, Beryl, Susan and Nigel".

Letter 29 January 1974

"Len

It is now Tuesday 29 January, I won't apologise because you know a bowler doesn't have much time to write letters at the weekend. In fact I have had a more active weekend than normal; Weston had us out practising for our big cricket match next w/end; the bowls section is playing the cricket section on Sunday morning at cricket and after a liquid lunch of approx two hours we will be having a game of bowls in the afternoon. Should there be no outright decision after the two games; a beer boat-race will decide the issue in the evening. However, I am not sure we will be able to raise a team after our exertions at practice. I have a torn hamstring, Aubrey has torn a muscle in his back, Robbie Mac has put his knee out of joint and Rodger has trapped his finger but won't say where.

I have just received your letter of the 25 January 1974 and I am very pleased to hear that you are now in full employment. I will be able to put everyone's minds at rest now and tell them you are not coming back after all. Beryl says have you found me a job yet? She says 'You lie my boy' about staying in every night in wicked London, but she won't tell Iris. I don't want to seem ignorant but where in London is Harpenden? I have never heard of it but I am sure it must be in the stockbroker belt.

Being in London it will be easier for you to see Weston and his band of Piss-Cat-Roses when they get there.

Best Wishes Ted".

Letter sent 12 July 1974

"Dear Len, This letter is more of an urgent appeal for help rather than an exchange of pleasantries. At a meeting of the 1976 UK Bowls Tour Members on Wednesday night I was asked in my capacity as Secretary of the tour to contact you and see if you can assist us with information re a possible itinerary for the tour.

What we want to know is where we can play bowls on a tour of England, Scotland and Wales. Our initial plans are that we travel up the East Coast playing bowls in Norfolk and Lincolnshire then on up to Edinburgh and Scotland. We would stay in Scotland for a few days, maybe a week and play bowls wherever we can, then we would move on down the West Coast stopping off in the Lake District. By the way do they play bowls in the Lake District? Then on down to South Wales, play bowls there and then down to the South Coast.

We expect the bowls side of the tour that is playing bowls and sightseeing to last approx 24-28 days and then at the end we would have 7-10 days free to do our thing.

What we would like from you Len, that is if you don't mind helping us, is could you find out for us fairly quickly where we will be able to play bowls on the above-mentioned route. We don't want you to have all the trouble of arranging games for us: we would write to the people concerned ourselves, except perhaps Harpenden Bowling Club, when by 1976 I expect you to be at least Chairman and you will be able personally organise that one for us.

Bob Dowie suggests that you could use his name and contact Jimmy Elms who is apparently the Secretary of the International Bowling Association. He would probably be a great help in suggesting names of clubs that we could contact.

You will appreciate Len that we would like to start writing to various clubs as soon as possible so that we can formulate an itinerary and get some hotel accommodation booked, with a party of 30-40 people, the hotel will probably be our biggest problem. One thing that may be a great help to me is a handbook with all the bowling clubs in it.

As you will gather by now our tour is beginning to take shape and I can tell you there is a great deal of enthusiasm being shown by the members. Here are some of the names that may interest you: The Dowies, The Joostes, The Fouries, The Bodensteins, The Macdonalds, The Lewins, The Symcoxes (Weston), The Moults, The Colyns, Henry West, Gerry Faulkner, Eddy Millar, Ken Marcus, Archie McLaren, Jimmy Gray and yours truly and his good lady. So you see we are a powerful combination and the opposition will have to be strong to give us a good game.

The dates of the tour will be June and July 1976. We have already started our fund-raising to pay for the bus to take us around the country so if you have a few bob to spare you could perhaps buy a few raffle tickets. Elsie is our fund raising 'Organiser in Chief' with Ben Bodenstein providing most of the prizes; that again is a powerful combination.

That's about all re-the bowls tour. You will do your best to help us with the necessary information won't you Len? Your former colleagues on the GW Executive, who shall remain nameless, said 'if anyone can get this information for us quickly Len Thompson can.'

Onto some interesting news for you. In the absence of Rodger, Claude, Weston and 'Len' Symcox, I managed to get a prize in the Winter Rinks this year. Our team of Fink Reddie, Henry West, Gerry Faulkner and myself were runners up to Alf, Jack, Brian

Waddington and Joe Charlton.

This year's competition was played all day Saturday and Sunday because the government decided to abolish Family Day. Out of the 24 teams entered no-one was unbeaten which was quite remarkable so the calculator was kind to us and we got second prize. Incidentally, believe it or not, they didn't have suitcases this year, we got woollen blankets.

Do you remember Brian Butler and his wife? He is a fitter at the Treatment Plant who used to be at Wesselton. Anyway, they went to England for a holiday at the beginning of June and he has come back on his own. Apparently his wife refused to return, so my wife is not the only one who thinks England is the place to be. I can almost hear Iris echoing Beryl's comment of 'Good for Mrs Butler.'

If you have any strength left Len after your parties with the Roses cricketers give all my love to Iris in the most practical way you can think of.

Best wishes, Ted".

Ted had written to me on the Friday 12 July, he died in the air crash on Tuesday 16 July, my friend Alex phoned me from South Africa while I was at work in London and I received Ted's letter two days later. How macabre! At least he was, no doubt, smiling when he wrote the last of the marvellous letters that we exchanged. God bless him.

Needless to say the 40 or so involved in the proposed Roses bowls tour were shattered by Ted's death and the tour was cancelled with sadness. No one could ever have taken Ted's place. Kimberley was a much sadder town for years after and, even now, I think of him, especially when I watch his favourite rugby league team 'St Helens' playing. I feel he is always with me, cheering them on to victory.

Unlike Iris, I hardly ever suffered from homesickness when in South Africa. I was normally far too busy for that to happen, except at Christmas and birthday times, when our parents were missed. Realistically though, looking back, a number of our objectives in going to South Africa had been achieved.

We had made many friends and the social life was certainly different. We had seen numerous landscapes and endured new climates. Our children did not have a smooth childhood but, when they look back, they maintain they had a very happy time in South Africa. In differing degrees, we all learned new languages like Afrikaans and my Zulu and Xhosa using Fanakalo. We met lots of challenges, succeeded with most of them and experienced an improving financial situation.

A disadvantage had been the amount of stress I suffered early on in the gold mines. However, after moving to De Beers, life became much more the way I had hoped it would and we had enough money to return home. We had travelled the length and breadth of South Africa and seen a large part of the country, including the wild animal parks. We had been to the capital cities of Johannesburg, Pretoria, Cape Town, and Bloemfontein besides Durban, Port Elizabeth and East London. We had visited the former British colony of Lesotho (Basutoland) and Swaziland. These trips gave us memories and images that would remain forever

It is said that reading and travelling broaden the mind, stimulate the imagination and provide a liberal education. I think we can rightly claim to have succeeded on all those points. Although the children suffered from their lapses in schooling due to following me around the mines it did not prevent them from becoming successful in their adult lives.

I am now seventy years old. When I left England in 1966 I said that I would be away for five years. I was to be gone for seven. Perhaps I did the wrong thing for Iris and the children. On the other hand we would not have had our daughter, Julia, had we not emigrated to South Africa. In that case we did the right thing. At least I had kept my promise to Iris and that surpassed all individual thoughts and misgivings.

Looking back, I had left an excellent job, a lot of friends and a very good way of life. However, external factors such as social position, wealth and popularity are not as important as honesty, sincerity, humility, generosity and readiness to serve our friends and family whenever we can. I could hear my dear old mam saying the same. Having left her for seven years, at least she could be proud of her son Lenny.

On a personal note, I have returned four times, including the visit this year to do my final research for this book. I am still overwhelmed by the hospitality, friendliness and the courtesies shown by the South African people, of all races, colours and creeds. If fate allows, I will return again to the land of my dreams.

In conclusion I feel that the seven years I spent in South Africa changed me from the 'rough diamond' I was when I arrived there to the polished individual I had become on my return to the UK.

Thank you South Africa.

Acknowledgements

FIRST OF ALL I would like to thank Patrick Leonard Symcox for being kind enough to write the foreword for this book. By doing so he has extended the link between myself and his father Rodger who was my best friend during our stay in Kimberley. As you maybe aware Patrick was highly successful as a South African cricketer. This was no doubt due to the encouragement and guidance from his Dad who performed similar feats whilst playing for De Beers Country Club and the best bowls coach I have come across.

I am also very grateful to all those who have contributed to these 'A Rough Diamond in South Africa' memories, to those who have supplied photographs, and to those who have helped in any way to produce this book.

I especially wish to thank my friend Peter Ashley from Chesterfield for doing most of the hard work in guiding me in all aspects of the production of the book and to my old school chums Des Baker and Marion Yeldham for reading the scripts along with my former boss Leslie Jones and wife Margaret.

A special mention for my cousins Delice and son Maxim Levenson for their guidance, support and enthusiasm for the project.

Special thanks go to Anglo American Corporation of South Africa and De Beers Consolidated Mines Limited for allowing me access to their vast archives and for them and the Kimberley Africana Library for supplying photographs from their records.

I am also indebted to my son Leon and his friend Mark 'McGinty' Adams for their help with the scanning of images, design and layout of the book.

Any discrepancy in any of the memories is entirely due to the passage of time.

Finally, a special word of gratitude to my wife Iris for her support during a very trying time when we are supposed to be enjoying the twilight of our lives.

If any reader wishes to ask any questions concerning the contents of the book please email me on len@sportsdraw.co.uk.

Bibliography

50 Years on the Diamond Fields 1870-1920 - Kokkie Duminy
A History of South Africa - Leonard Thompson
Burgers Daughter - Nadine Gordimer
Cullinan Diamonds Dreams and Discoveries - Phillida Brooke Simons
De Beers News - De Beers Consolidated Mines Limited
Diamond People - AJ Wannenburgh & Peter Johnson
Diamonds Famous & Fatal - Leo Kendall
Essential Gesture - Nadine Gordimer
Every Secret Thing - Gillian Slovo
Mandela - Anthony Sampson
News from the Mines - De Beers Consolidated Mines Limited
Rainbow Nation Revisited - Donald Woods
Reef Magazine - South African Chamber of Mines Services
Somewhere Over the Rainbow - Gavin Bell
The Big Five Mines of Kimberley - Steve Lunderstedt
The Making of South Africa - Aran S MacKinnon
Tribal Life in South Africa - Frameworthy Publications
Washing of the Spears - Donald R Morris
Welkom - Felstar Publishers

List of Contributors

Iris, Leon, Andrew and Julia Thompson
Alex and Jean Lewin
Sandra and Weston Symcox
Bill and Ross Bartholomew
Moira, Elaine and Kim Burgess
Mike and Ann Doherty
Mary-Lynn du Toit (nee Le Barrow) and David
Eddie Green
Gerry Claughton
Willie Boshoff
Giel Venter
Erhard Du Toit
Kokkie Duminy
Louise Erasmus
Elsie Fourie
Norman Goosen
Beryl, Susan and Nigel Hall

Shereen Maytham
Charmaine McClean
Archie Miller
Mike Nayler
Nicky Oppenheimer
Barrie Owen
John Pinder
Erna Robertson
Ingrid Henrici
Linda Symcox
Pat Symcox
Gillian and Naas Vermaak
Jean Waddington
Mervyn Ward
Dick & Myrtle Wilson
Carien Woodburne
Peter Ashley
Harold Barlow
Arthur McKenzie